MATERNAL CARE AND MENTAL HEALTH

A report prepared on behalf of the World Health Organization
as a contribution to the United Nations programme
for the welfare of homeless children

JOHN BOWLBY, M.A., M.D.

Director, Child Guidance Department, Tavistock Clinic, London
Consultant in Mental Health, World Health Organization

WORLD HEALTH ORGANIZATION
PALAIS DES NATIONS
GENEVA
1952

First impression, March 1951
Second impression, August 1951
Third impression, March 1952

Second edition, May 1952

Originally published in the *Bulletin of the World Health Organization*, 1951, **3**, 355-534.
Thereafter, issued in separate editions in English and in French in the Monograph Series
of the World Health Organization.

CONTENTS

TABLES

PREFACE TO SECOND EDITION

It is pleasing that the welcome given to the first edition of this monograph should so soon have necessitated a second. It remains unchanged apart from minor textual corrections, and the addition of an index.

In the meantime the plea for further research made in chapter 6 has not gone unheeded ; the International Children's Centre, Paris, is now supporting such research both in England and France. The Centre has also done much to further a wider understanding of the effects of maternal deprivation by the international seminars which it has sponsored. It is to be hoped that other bodies interested in research will follow its example.

February 1952   JOHN BOWLBY

PREFACE TO FIRST EDITION

At the third session of the Social Commission of the United Nations, held in April 1948, it was decided to make a study of the needs of homeless children.[143] These were described as " children who are orphaned or separated from their families for other reasons and need care in foster homes, institutions or other types of group care ". The study was to be confined to " children who were homeless in their native country ", thus explicitly excluding refugees from war or other disaster. When the specialized agencies interested in the matter were approached by the United Nations for their comments and suggestions, the World Health Organization offered to contribute a study of the mental health aspects of the problem. This offer was accepted and has resulted in the present report.

I took up my temporary appointment with the World Health Organization in January 1950, and during the late winter and early spring visited several countries in Europe—France, the Netherlands, Sweden, Switzerland, and the United Kingdom—and the United States of America. In each I had discussions with workers, most of whom were concerned with child care and child guidance, saw something of their work, and was introduced to the literature. In these discussions I found a very high degree of agreement existing both in regard to the principles underlying the mental health of children and the practices by which it may be safeguarded. In compiling this report my task has thus been to do justice to an extensive literature and to bring out the many points of importance to which my attention has been drawn ; little time has had to be expended in reconciling divergent views.

A word of explanation is needed in regard to the large number of figures and tables which I have quoted. In almost every case the tables appearing in this report have either been constructed from data not available in tabular form or represent simplifications of tables given in the original papers. Moreover, in a number of cases where tests of significance had not been done on data which were nevertheless adequate for testing, I have had them calculated, using the chi-square method.

It will be obvious that I am indebted for help to a wide circle of colleagues in many countries and I take this opportunity to thank them for so generously giving me of their time and hospitality and making my tour so profitable and enjoyable. I also wish to thank my many correspondents for replying so promptly to my requests for reports and information. It has unfortunately not been possible to make full use of much of the material

I have been given, and my difficulty in doing justice to publications in languages other than English has been a source of particular concern. While it has been my endeavour to cover all the literature on the adverse effects of maternal deprivation, the subject of Part I, I am aware of many omissions in my references to the literature on family and child care, which is now very large. My aim in the second part of this report has been rather to deal with certain special aspects of the subject which have tended to be neglected.

My gratitude is due, too, to the North West Metropolitan Regional Hospital Board and the Management Committee responsible for the Tavistock Clinic for giving me leave of absence for this work with WHO, and also to my colleagues at the Clinic who shouldered extra burdens to enable me to undertake it.

Many of the concepts contained in Part I have been clarified in discussion during the past two years with members of a research team at the Tavistock Clinic which has for its aim the study of the effects on personality development of separation from the mother in early childhood. To the Sir Halley Stewart Trust which initiated this project, and to Mr. James Robertson, Miss Mary Flanders, and Dr. Dugmore Hunter who have taken part in it and have assisted me in numerous ways, I owe especial thanks. In particular, I would like to thank Mr. Eric Trist of the Tavistock Institute of Human Relations who has also taken part in the planning of this project and whose theoretical insight and wide knowledge have been of the greatest value to me over many years.

Finally, I should like to thank Dr. Ronald Hargreaves, Chief of the Mental Health Section of the World Health Organization, for his help in planning my visits and discovering the literature, and for much personal kindness, and M. Philippe Kocher, his research assistant, for abstracting many papers and books.

October 1950   JOHN BOWLBY

Part I

ADVERSE EFFECTS OF MATERNAL DEPRIVATION

CHAPTER 1

SOME ORIGINS OF MENTAL ILL-HEALTH

Among the most significant developments in psychiatry during the past
quarter of a century has been the steady growth of evidence that the quality
of the parental care which a child receives in his earliest years is of vital
importance for his future mental health. Such evidence came first from
the psycho-analytic treatment of adults and then from that of children.
It has been greatly amplified during the past decade by information gathered
by psychologists and psychiatrists working in child guidance and child
care—two fields affording unrivalled opportunities for first-hand observation both of the developing child and of his milieu.

Largely as a result of this new knowledge, there is today a high level of
agreement among child-guidance workers in Europe and America on
certain central concepts. Their approach to cases, their investigations,
their diagnostic criteria, and their therapeutic aims are the same. Above
all, the theory of etiology on which their work is founded is the same.

The basic principles of this theory of the origins of mental health and
mental illness will be discussed more fully later. For the moment it is
sufficient to say that what is believed to be essential for mental health is
that the infant and young child should experience a warm, intimate, and
continuous relationship with his mother (or permanent mother-substitute)
in which both find satisfaction and enjoyment. Given this relationship,
the emotions of anxiety and guilt, which in excess characterize mental ill-
health, will develop in a moderate and organized way. When this happens,
the child's characteristic and contradictory demands, on the one hand for
unlimited love from his parents and on the other for revenge upon them
when he feels that they do not love him enough, will likewise remain of
moderate strength and become amenable to the control of his gradually
developing personality. It is this complex, rich, and rewarding relationship with the mother in the early years, varied in countless ways by relations
with the father and with siblings, that child psychiatrists and many others
now believe to underlie the development of character and of mental health.

A state of affairs in which the child does not have this relationship is
termed ' maternal deprivation '. This is a general term covering a number
of different situations. Thus, a child is deprived even though living at
home if his mother (or permanent mother-substitute) is unable to give him
the loving care small children need. Again, a child is deprived if for any

reason he is removed from his mother's care. This deprivation will be relatively mild if he is then looked after by someone whom he has already learned to know and trust, but may be considerable if the foster-mother, even though loving, is a stranger. All these arrangements, however, give the child some satisfaction and are therefore examples of partial deprivation. They stand in contrast to the almost complete deprivation which is still not uncommon in institutions, residential nurseries, and hospitals, where the child often has no one person who cares for him in a personal way and with whom he may feel secure.

The ill-effects of deprivation vary with its degree. Partial deprivation brings in its train acute anxiety, excessive need for love, powerful feelings of revenge, and, arising from these last, guilt and depression. These emotions and drives are too great for the immature means of control and organization available to the young child (immature physiologically as well as psychologically). The consequent disturbance of psychic organization then leads to a variety of responses, often repetitive and cumulative, the end products of which are symptoms of neurosis and instability of character. Complete deprivation, with which we shall be dealing principally in this report, has even more far-reaching effects on character development and may entirely cripple the capacity to make relationships.

The evidence on which these views are based is largely clinical in origin. Immensely valuable though this evidence is, it is unfortunately neither systematic nor statistically controlled, and so has frequently met with scepticism from those not engaged in child psychiatry.

Investigators with a statistical bent have worked with the concept of the ' broken home ' and a number of studies have demonstrated a relation between maladjustment and this situation. As an example an extensive study undertaken by Menut[101] may be quoted. He compared 839 children suffering from behaviour disorders with nearly 70,000 controls from the schools of Paris, and found that of the problem children 66% came from broken homes while of the controls only 12% did so. In a subsequent more detailed study of 100 of the problem children from broken homes he assessed the broken home itself as being a main causative factor in 84. A review of similar studies is given in Appendix 1.[a]

But though these studies have been of value in amplifying and confirming clinical evidence of the far-reaching importance of the child's early experience in his home, the concept of the broken home is scientifically unsatisfactory and should be abandoned. It includes too many heterogeneous conditions having very different psychological effects.

In place of the concept of the broken home we need to put the concept of the disturbed parent-child relationship which is frequently, but not necessarily, associated with it. If the child's developing relationships with

a See page 161.

his mother and his father are used as the focal point, data of far greater precision emerge, and much that is obscure in the origins of mental illness begins to become clear. An illustration of the fruitfulness of this stand-point is a recent study by Stott,[137] who has published the full case-histories of 102 persistent offenders aged between 15 and 18 years who were in an English Approved School. In this comparatively large series he has demon-strated clearly how anxieties arising from unsatisfactory relationships in early childhood predispose the children to respond in an antisocial way to later stresses. Most of the early anxiety situations noted by Stott are particular aspects of maternal deprivation.

Naturally, parent-child relationships have many dimensions and there are many other ways besides deprivation, arising from separation or outright rejection, in which they may become pathogenic. The commonest are (a) an unconsciously rejecting attitude underlying a loving one, (b) an excessive demand for love and reassurance on the part of a parent, and (c) a parent obtaining unconscious and vicarious satisfaction from the child's beha-viour, despite conscious condemnation of it. These themes, however, do not concern this report ; nor does it treat in detail the child's relation to his father. The reason for this is that almost all the evidence concerns the child's relation to his mother, which is without doubt in ordinary circum-stances by far his most important relationship during these years. It is she who feeds and cleans him, keeps him warm, and comforts him. It is to his mother that he turns when in distress. In the young child's eyes father plays second fiddle and his value increases only as the child's vulnerability to deprivation decreases. Nevertheless, as the illegitimate child knows, fathers have their uses even in infancy. Not only do they provide for their wives to enable them to devote themselves unrestrictedly to the care of the infant and toddler, but, by providing love and companionship, they support her emotionally and help her maintain that harmonious contented mood in the aura of which the infant thrives. In what follows, therefore, while continual reference will be made to the mother-child relation, little will be said of the father-child relation ; his value as the economic and emotional support of the mother will be assumed.

Theories which place the origins of mental disturbances in these intimate domestic events are, of course, in strong contrast to the theories which stem from the German school of psychiatry. These stress constitutional and inherited factors, at times to a point reminiscent of Calvinistic predestina-tion. Suffice it to say that evidence for these extreme views does not exist and that the relative weights of nature and nurture remain still to be deter-mined. In this connexion, it is useful to remember that recent work in embryology has produced a steady accumulation of evidence that patho-logical changes in the embryo's environment may cause faults of growth and development exactly resembling those that in the past have been ascribed to pure genetic causes.[45] This is a finding of great importance, which, as will be seen, is exactly paralleled in psychology. It is to be emphasized, however, that such findings in no way contradict theories postulating the adverse influence of hereditary factors, except in so far as these are held in the extreme form that hereditary factors alone account for all differences in human behaviour. Indeed, all those subscribing to the views set out in this report believe that in the final analysis hereditary factors will be shown also to play a part and that the greatest scientific progress will be made when the interaction of the two can be studied.

A second far-reaching biological principle also stems from embryology, namely, the discovery that the harmful effects on the embryo of trauma, intoxication, infection, and other potentially damaging processes vary not only with the nature of the offending agent and the structure and function of the tissue mainly attacked but also with the maturity of that tissue. In the psychological field this principle is illustrated in the now classic work of Hunt,[79] who demonstrated experimentally that the starvation of rats on the 24th day of life left traces on behaviour clearly discernible in adult life, while a similar experience at 36 days had no such effect.

Finally, it may be noted that in the physiological sphere it has been observed that the evil effects on an organ are especially far-reaching when noxious influences operate during its earliest phases of development, as for instance in the case of rubella where maximal damage is caused between the sixth and tenth weeks of foetal life. The identity of the biological principle at work here and that invoked by psychiatrists who impute far-reaching effects to certain emotional experiences occurring in the earliest phases of mental functioning, as early as the first six months of life, will be apparent. It may be said, therefore, that these theories, so far from being inherently improbable, are strictly in accord with accepted biological principle.

CHAPTER 2

REVIEW OF EVIDENCE ON EFFECTS OF DEPRIVATION
I : DIRECT STUDIES

Classes of Evidence

Evidence that the deprivation of mother-love in early childhood can have a far-reaching effect on the mental health and personality development of human beings comes from many sources. It falls into three main classes :

(a) Studies, by direct observation, of the mental health and development of children in institutions, hospitals, and foster-homes—direct studies.

(b) Studies which investigate the early histories of adolescents or adults who have developed psychological illnesses—retrospective studies.

(c) Studies which follow up groups of children who have suffered deprivation in their early years with a view to determining their state of mental health —follow-up studies.

The extent to which these studies, undertaken by people of many nations, varied training and, as often as not, ignorant of each others' conclusions, confirm and support each other is impressive. What each individual piece of work lacks in thoroughness, scientific reliability, or precision is largely made good by the concordance of the whole. Nothing in scientific method carries more weight than this. Divergent voices are few. Indeed, only three have come to light, all follow-up studies, but of a quality which bears no comparison with that of the research the conclusions of which they challenge.

The direct studies are the most numerous. They make it plain that, when deprived of maternal care, the child's development is almost always retarded—physically, intellectually, and socially—and that symptoms of physical and mental illness may appear. Such evidence is disquieting, but sceptics may question whether the retardation is permanent and whether the symptoms of illness may not easily be overcome. The retrospective and follow-up studies make it clear that such optimism is not always justified and that some children are gravely damaged for life. This is a sombre conclusion which must now be regarded as established.

There are, however, important features of the situation about which little is known. For instance, it is by no means clear why some children succumb and some do not. It may be that hereditary factors play a part, but, before resorting to a principle which has been so readily invoked as a universal solvent of biological problems, it is important to review what is known of the effects of such factors as the child's age, and the length and, especially, the degree of his deprivation, each of which there is reason to think is vital.

The three classes of evidence will now be reviewed, attention being paid throughout to data which may help towards an understanding of the role played by these three factors.

Direct Studies

Direct observations of the ill-effects on young children of complete deprivation of maternal care have been made by a large number of paediatricians, psychologists, and child psychiatrists and have shown that the child's development may be affected physically, intellectually, emotionally, and socially. All children under about seven years of age seem to be vulnerable and some of the effects are clearly discernible within the first few weeks of life.

Bakwin [7, 8] and Ribble [120] have each given detailed accounts of the adverse effects on physical health. Bakwin,[8] who gives a valuable survey of the paediatric literature on the subject which goes back at least to 1909, summarizes his own observations thus :

" Infants under 6 months of age who have been in an institution for some time present a well-defined picture. The outstanding features are listlessness, emaciation and pallor, relative immobility, quietness, unresponsiveness to stimuli like a smile or a coo, indifferent appetite, failure to gain weight properly despite the ingestion of diets which, in the home, are entirely adequate, frequent stools, poor sleep, an appearance of unhappiness, proneness to febrile episodes, absence of sucking habits. "

These changes, he remarks, are not observable in the first 2-4 weeks of life, but can be seen any time thereafter, sometimes within a few days of the baby's separation from his mother. The failure of such babies to smile at the sight of a human face has been confirmed experimentally by Spitz & Wolf [135] while Gesell & Amatruda [57] have noted a diminished interest and reactivity to be characteristic as early as 8-12 weeks. A very careful study of the infant's babbling and crying by Brodbeck & Irwin [30] showed that babies from birth to six months in an orphanage were consistently less vocal than those in families, the difference being clearly discernible before two months of age. As will be seen, this backwardness in ' talking ' is especially characteristic of the institution child of all ages.

This diverse evidence from reputable workers leaves no room for doubt that the development of the institution infant deviates from the norm at a very early age. If the regime is continued, the deviations become more pronounced. Gesell & Amatruda have listed their appearance (see table I).

These findings, while giving more detail, confirm in principle those of such early workers in the field as Ripin,[123] Vance, Prall, Simpson

TABLE I. ORDER OF APPEARANCE OF ADVERSE REACTIONS IN INSTITUTION INFANTS (GESELL & AMATRUDA)

Adverse reactions	Time of appearance
Diminished interest and reactivity	8 — 12 weeks
Reduced integration of total behaviour	8 — 12 weeks
Beginning of retardation evidenced by disparity between exploitation in supine and in sitting positions	12 — 16 weeks
Excessive preoccupation with strange persons.	12 — 16 weeks
General retardation (prone behaviour relatively unaffected).	24 — 28 weeks
Blandness of facial expression	24 — 28 weeks
Impoverished initiative	24 — 28 weeks
Channelization and stereotypies of sensori-motor behaviour	24 — 28 weeks
Ineptness in new social situations	44 — 48 weeks
Exaggerated resistance to new situations	48 — 52 weeks
Relative retardation in language behaviour	12 — 15 months

& McLaughlin (reported by Jones & Burks[85]), and Durfee & Wolf.[50] Using the Hetzer-Wolf baby tests, the latter compared the developmental quotients (DQ)[b] of 118 infants in various institutions and correlated their findings with the amount of maternal care which the infants received. Although they discerned no differences before the age of three months, differences steadily increased so that the children who had been institutionalized for more than eight months during the first year showed such severe psychiatric disturbances that they could not be tested.

Spitz,[133] with Wolf, using the same tests, has more recently made a systematic study of the adverse effects which occur during the first year if the child is kept throughout in an institutional environment. They studied altogether four groups of children, in three of which the babies were with their mothers and one where they were not. Though the absolute levels of development, not unexpectedly, differed according to the social group the babies came from, there was no change of quotient during the year in the case of the babies, 103 in all, who lived with their mothers. The group of 61 brought up in an hygienic institution, on the other hand, showed a catastrophic drop of developmental quotient between the ages of 4 and 12 months. This is shown in table II.

At the earlier age the average DQ was 124 and second in magnitude of the four groups. By 12 months it had sunk to 72 and was by far the lowest. By the end of the second year it had sunk to 45. The last two figures indicate grave retardation.

In confirmation of earlier work, Spitz & Wolf's results show that most of the drop in DQ had taken place during the first six months of life.

---

b The developmental quotient, although calculated in a way similar to the intelligence quotient (IQ), is concerned with general physical and mental development, of which intelligence is only a part. A DQ of 90-110 represents average development.

TABLE II. MEAN DEVELOPMENTAL QUOTIENT OF INFANTS AT BEGINNING AND END OF FIRST YEAR WITH REGARD TO SOCIAL CLASS AND TO EXPERIENCE (SPITZ)

Social class	Presence or absence of mother	Number of cases	Developmental quotient	
			Average of 1st to 4th months	Average of 9th to 12th months
Unselected urban	absent	61	124	72
Professional . . .	present	23	133	131
Peasant	present	11	107	108
Delinquent unmarried mothers . .	present	69	101.5	105

It is true that these infants were living in conditions especially bad from the psychological point of view, as not only was there but one nurse to some seven children, but, for reasons of hygiene, the children were kept restricted to cots and cubicles in what amounted to solitary confinement. However, studies such as those of Rheingold [119] and Levy [92] make it plain that retardation may occur in conditions which are far from being as adverse as these. Rheingold studied 29 children aged from 6 months to 2½ years (mostly between 9 and 15 months) all of whom were awaiting adoption. All had been cared for by foster-mothers ; 15 with no other young children, the remainder with up to three others in the same foster-home. Those receiving all the foster-mother's attention were on the average accelerated in development while those who had to share it with other babies were retarded to a statistically significant degree. Levy also studied infants awaiting adoption. Her main sample was composed of 122 babies, 83 cared for in an institution and 39 in foster-homes, all of whom had come into the agency's care within their first two months of life, and had been tested around six months of age. Those in the institution were in one large nursery, which had accommodation for 17 babies and was staffed by a total of 10 practical nurses, there never being fewer than two in attendance during the day. The DQs on Gesell tests are shown to be slightly above average for the foster-home children and slightly below for the institution-alized, a difference which is staitstically significant. Unfortunately, neither Rheingold nor Levy give their results in a form comparable to those of Spitz & Wolf, but it is clear that the drop in DQ in Levy's institutional group is far less than that of the group studied by Spitz & Wolf, a result which no doubt reflects the better psychological conditions in which they lived.

There are several studies showing similar retardation in *the second and later years*. One of the earliest was that of Gindl et al. [58] who, working in prewar Vienna, showed a difference of 10 points in mean DQ between a group of 20 children aged from 15 to 23 months who had spent six months or more in an institution and a similar group brought up in the poorest of homes. Confirmation comes from Denmark, France, and the USA.

Goldfarb,[68] in a very thorough study of 30 children aged 34-35 months, half of whom had lived in an institution and the other half in foster-homes from four months of age, found a difference of 28 points of IQ on the Stanford-Binet test between the two groups. The IQs of the foster-home group averaged 96, which is average, those of the institution children 68, which is seriously retarded and borders on mentally defective. The difference on the Merrill-Palmer test was less dramatic but none the less serious, figures being 91 and 79 respectively.

Simonsen,[130] using the Hetzer-Bühler tests, compared a group of 113 children, aged between one and four years, almost all of whom had spent their whole lives in one of some 12 different institutions, with a comparable group who lived at home and attended day nurseries. The mothers of these children were working and the homes often very unsatisfactory. Even so, the average DQ of the family children was normal—102—while that of the institution children retarded—93. This difference is found consistently at each of three age-levels, namely, children in the second, third, and fourth years of life.

TABLE III. COMPARATIVE DQs AND IQs OF INSTITUTION AND FAMILY CHILDREN AGED FROM ONE TO FOUR YEARS

Investigators	Tests	Time spent in institution	DQs/IQs	
			institution group	family group
Gindl et al.	Hetzer-Bühler	at least 6 months	90	100
Goldfarb	Stanford-Binet Merrill-Palmer	from about 4 months	68 79	96 91
Simonsen	Hetzer-Bühler	from birth	93	102
Roudinesco & Appell	Gesell	at least 2 months	59	95

Finally, Roudinesco & Appell [126] are at present making a similar study in Paris, taking as their sample children, also aged from one to four years, who have spent two months or more in an institution. This group numbers 40. The control group of 104 children of similar age and social class is drawn from nursery schools situated in poor districts. Using the Gesell tests, they found that the average DQ of the children living with their families was 95, that of the institution children as low as 59. As in Simonsen's study, the adverse effects seem to obtain throughout the age-range, though their numbers are still rather small for firm conclusions to be drawn. An important finding confirming the work of Durfee & Wolf and of Spitz & Wolf, though in this case it refers to an older age-group, is that the longer the child is in the institution, the lower becomes the DQ. Although numbers in each subgroup are small, totalling between 12 and 30, the consistency of the finding in each of the subtests suggests its reliability. The overall DQ drops from about 65 for those who have been in for between two and six months to about 50 for those in for more than a year.

These four studies from four different countries using as criteria four different tests are remarkably consistent. In each case the quotient of the control group averages about 100 while that of the institution group is retarded, very seriously so in the cases of Goldfarb and of Roudinesco & Appell. The results are conveniently tabulated in table III.

Although the results of tests of statistical significance are given only by Goldfarb, the internal consistency of the results of both Simonsen and of Roudinesco & Appell make it clear that in neither case can the results be due merely to chance.

So far only the overall scores on tests of development (Hetzer-Bühler and Gesell) and of intelligence (Standford-Binet and Merrill-Palmer) have been used as criteria. Studies, however, show that not all aspects of development are equally affected. The least affected is neuromuscular development, including walking, other locomotor activities, and manual dexterity. The most affected is speech, the ability to express being more retarded than the ability to understand. (Speech retardation is sometimes made good remarkably quickly, Burlingham & Freud [39] reporting that " when children are home on visits ... they sometimes gain in speech in one or two weeks what they would have taken three months to gain in the nursery "). Midway in retardation between motor development and speech come social responses and what Gesell calls ' adaptivity '. Here again there is remarkable agreement between a number of different workers, among whom may be mentioned Gindl et al., Goldfarb (who gave special attention to speech), Burlingham & Freud, Simonsen, and Roudinesco & Appell.

Though there can be no mistaking the consistency of these findings, their import is frequently questioned on the grounds that many children in institutions are born of parents of poor stock, physically and mentally, and that heredity alone might well account for all the differences. Those who advance this objection do not seem to be aware that in the majority of the studies quoted care has been taken by the investigators to ensure that the control groups, brought up either in their own homes or in foster-homes, are of a similar social class and, as nearly as possible, spring from similar stock. Explicit data on this point are given by Brodbeck & Irwin,[30] Levy,[92] Spitz,[133] and Goldfarb,[66] while in the cases of Gindl et al.,[58] Rheingold,[119] Simonsen,[130] and Roudinesco & Appell,[126] sufficient care has been taken on the point to make it most improbable that heredity accounts for all the variation. Even so the only certain method of controlling heredity is by the use of a sample of identical twins. Though there are no human twin studies of the problem, Liddell (personal communication) is doing experimental work on twin goat kids, one of whom is separated from its mother for a brief spell each day and the other not. Except for the daily experimental period of 40 minutes, both kids live with and feed from their mother. During the experimental period the lights are periodically extinguished, a stimulus known to create anxiety in goats, and this produces very different behaviour in the twins. The one which is with its mother is at ease and moves around freely ; the isolated one is " psychologically frozen " (Liddell's words) and remains cowed in a corner. In one of the first experiments the isolated kid discontinued suckling from its mother and, the experimenters being unaware of this and so unable to help, died of dehydration after a few days. This is ample demonstration of the adverse effects of maternal deprivation on the mammalian young, and disposes finally of the argument that all the observed effects are due to heredity.

Moreover, positive evidence that the causative factor is maternal deprivation comes from innumerable sources. First, there are the very clear findings of Durfee & Wolf, of Spitz & Wolf, and of Roudinesco & Appell that the longer the deprivation, the lower falls the DQ. Secondly, there is experimental evidence that even if the child remains in the same institution, extra mothering from a substitute will diminish the ill-effects. Nearly twenty years ago Daniels studied two groups of two-year olds living in the same institution. " One group was given very little tenderness although adequately cared for in every other respect ", while in the other " a nurse was assigned to each child and there was no lack of tenderness and affection. At the end of half a year the first group was mentally and physically retarded, in comparison with the second." [c]

A comparable experiment has been done by Roudinesco & Appell [126] who arranged that each of 11 children, of ages ranging from 19 months to 3 years and 8 months, should have special attention comprising four sessions a week of three-quarters of an hour each with a special member of staff (in 10 cases the psychologist, in 1 case a nurse). Though in some cases therapeutic work was attempted, for most the session consisted of giving the child a chance of regular contact, away from the others, with a sympathetic adult. In several cases the results were very satisfactory. For instance, one child, whose DQ had fallen to 37 and had later (aged 18 months) become untestable, improved to 70 after three months of this treatment, and another of $2\frac{1}{2}$ years, whose DQ had also fallen very low and had become untestable, improved to 100 (average) after a year's work.

---

c Reported by Bühler.[34] It is not clear whether in the second group each child had a separate nurse which the text implies, or whether each child was assigned to a nurse, which seems more likely.

Finally, there is the evidence of spectacular changes in the child's condition following restoration to his mother. Bakwin,[7] after recording the views of the older generation of paediatricians, himself remarks :

" The rapidity with which the symptoms of hospitalism begin to disappear when an afflicted baby is placed in a good home is amazing. It is convincing evidence of the etiologic relation of the emotionally arid atmosphere of the hospital to the symptoms. The baby promptly becomes more animated and responsive ; fever, if present in the hospital, disappears in twenty-four to seventy-two hours ; there is a gain in weight and an improvement in the color."

He cites as an example a boy who at four months of age, the latter two in hospital, weighed less than at birth and whose condition was critical.

" His appearance was that of a pale, wrinkled old man. His breathing was so weak and superficial that it seemed as though he might stop breathing at any moment. When seen twenty-four hours after he had been at home he was cooing and smiling. Though no change had been made in his diet he started to gain promptly and by the end of the first year his weight was well within the normal range. He appeared to be in every way a normal child."

The dramatic and tragic changes in behaviour and feeling which follow separation of the young child from his mother and the beneficent results of restoring him to her are in fact available for all to see and it is astonishing that so little attention has been given to them hitherto. So painful, indeed, are the agonies which these children suffer on separation that it may well be that those who have their care shut their eyes in self-protection. Yet of their existence there can be no doubt, as distressingly similar pictures are given by numerous different investigators.

Bakwin's description of the typical separated infant—listless, quiet, unhappy, and unresponsive to a smile or a coo—has already been quoted. This clinical picture, in the age-range of 6 to 12 months, has been the subject of systematic study by Spitz & Wolf,[134] who named it ' anaclitic depression '. And depression it undoubtedly is, having many of the hallmarks of the typical adult depressive patient of the mental hospital. The emotional tone is one of apprehension and sadness, there is a withdrawal from the environment amounting to rejection of it, there is no attempt to contact a stranger and no brightening if this stranger contacts him. Activities are retarded and the child often sits or lies inert in a dazed stupor. Insomnia is common and lack of appetite universal. Weight is lost and the child becomes prone to intercurrent infections. The drop in DQ is precipitous.

In what conditions, it may be asked, does this syndrome develop ? In general, it is characteristic of infants who have had a happy relationship with their mothers up till six or nine months and are then suddenly separated from them without an adequate substitute being provided. Of 95 children studied by Spitz & Wolf and on whom a diagnosis was made, 20% reacted to separation by severe depression and another 27% by mild depression making nearly 50% in all.[d] Almost all those with a close and loving relation

d In the original paper another 28 children are shown as " undiagnosed ". Subsequent study, it is understood, showed a large number of these cases to fall in the category of " severe depression " so that the figures quoted here are underestimates.

to their mothers suffered, which means that the depressive response to separation is a normal one at this age. The fact that a majority of those with unhappy relationships escaped indicates that their psychic development is already damaged and their later capacity for love likely to be impaired. The illness respected neither sex nor race—boys and girls, white and coloured, all being affected. Although recovery is rapid if the child is restored to his mother, the possibility of psychic scars which may later be reactivated cannot be disregarded, while, if the condition is permitted to continue, recovery is greatly impeded. Spitz & Wolf believe that there is a qualitative change after three months of deprivation, after which recovery is rarely, if ever, complete.

Spitz & Wolf report (verbal communication) that disturbances of development may also follow separation at an even earlier age. These disturbances are much less dramatic than in older babies and were at first described as ' mild depressions ', but further observation made this term seem wholly inappropriate since it became evident that the condition was neither mild nor, in the view of Spitz & Wolf, could it properly be classified as depression. These disturbances, to which infants of the age-group three to six months are prone, are insidious in development and much less easily reversed by restoration to the mother. The DQ falls slowly but steadily (not precipitously as in the older babies), and recovery is only partial—perhaps 25%-30% of the drop—instead of almost complete.

These very adverse results, it must be emphasized, can be partially avoided during the first year of life by the children being mothered by a substitute. Hitherto many have thought that substitute care could be completely successful during most of this year. Ribble [120] has expressed doubts, however, and Spitz & Wolf (verbal communication) are now definitely of the opinion that damage is frequently done by changes even as early as three months. Nevertheless, all are agreed that substitute care, even if not wholly adequate, is indispensable and should on no account be withheld. In the second and third years of life, the emotional response to separation is not only just as severe but substitute mothers are often rejected out of hand, the child becoming acutely and inconsolably distressed for a period of days, a week, or even more, without a break. During much of this time he is in a state of agitated despair and either screaming or moaning. Food and comfort are alike refused. Only exhaustion brings sleep. After some days he becomes quieter and may relapse into apathy, from which he slowly emerges to make a more positive response to his strange environment. For some weeks or even months, however, he may show a serious regression to infantile modes of behaviour. He wets his bed, masturbates, gives up talking, and insists on being carried, so that the less experienced nurse may suppose him to be defective.[e]

---

[e] Description based on unpublished observations of Robertson of the Tavistock Clinic, London.

Naturally there are very many variations of reaction in this age-group and not all children respond in the way described ; and once again it appears to be the children who have had the most intimate and happy relationship with their mothers who suffer most. Those who have been brought up in institutions and have had no permanent mother-figure show no responses of this kind at all, the result of their affective life already having been damaged. Though the inexperienced nurse welcomes the child who regards one adult as being as good as another and criticizes the family baby who reacts violently as having been ' spoilt ', all the evidence suggests that the violent reaction is normal and the apathetic resignation a sign of pathological development.

Those who are reluctant to admit the reality and potential seriousness of these reactions often express the belief that a little wise management can easily avoid them. Though much further research is required, there is good reason for believing that the prevention of such responses is very difficult. It is common knowledge that children in their second and third years in hospital are acutely upset after being visited by their parents, and skilled efforts to avoid this happening do not meet with success.[129] Moreover, Burlingham & Freud, who had several years' experience of these problems while running a residential nursery in Hampstead during the second World War, and who made every effort to make the transition from home to nursery easy for the child, were by no means always successful. In one of their monthly reports,[40] they write :

" In dealing with new cases of this kind we have attempted to work out a process of ' separation in slow stages ' so as to mitigate its consequences for the child. Though this has proved beneficial with children from three or four years onward, we have found that *very little can be done to prevent regression where children between 1 1/2 and 2 1/2 are concerned.* Infants of that age can stand sudden changes and separations of a day's length without any visible effect. Whenever it is more than that they tend to lose their emotional ties, revert in their instincts and regress in their behaviour " (authors' italics).

They illustrate this difficulty by giving a full account (written by Hellman) of the behaviour of a boy of 24 months who was a well-developed easy child with a good relation to his mother. Despite being looked after by the same mother-substitute and being visited daily by his mother during the first week of his stay, his behaviour deteriorated when she diminished her visits to two a week, and when she gave up visiting he regressed severely.

" He became listless, often sat in a corner sucking and dreaming, at other times he was very aggressive. He almost completely stopped talking. He was dirty and wet continually, so that we had to put nappies on him. He sat in front of his plate eating very little, without pleasure, and started smearing his food over the table. At this time the nurse who had been looking after him fell ill, and Bobby did not make friends with anyone else, but let himself be handled by everyone without opposition. A few days later he had tonsillitis and went to the sickroom. In the quiet atmosphere there he seemed not quite so unhappy, played quietly, but generally gave the impression of a baby. He hardly ever said a word, had entirely lost his bladder and bowel control, sucked a great deal. On his return to the nursery he looked very pale and tired. He was very unhappy after rejoining the group, always in trouble and in need of help and comfort. He did not seem to recognize the nurse who had looked after him at first."

The long-term after-effects on children of these harrowing experiences can sometimes be calamitous and are discussed later. The immediate after-effects, although not always evident to the untrained observer, are also frequently very disquieting to the psychiatrist. Those most commonly observed are (a) a hostile reaction to the mother on her return, which sometimes takes the form of a refusal to recognize her, (b) an excessive demandingness towards the mother or substitute mother, in which intense possessiveness is combined with intolerance of frustration, acute jealousy, and violent temper tantrums, (c) a cheerful but shallow attachment to any adult within the child's orbit, and (d) an apathetic withdrawal from all emotional entanglements, combined with monotonous rocking of the body and sometimes head banging. These reactions have been observed by many clinicians but are nowhere more vividly described than in the two publications of Burlingham & Freud.[38, 39]

A special note of warning must be sounded regarding the children who respond apathetically or by a cheerful undiscriminating friendliness, since people ignorant of the principles of mental health are habitually deceived by them. Often they are quiet, obedient, easy to manage, well-mannered and orderly, and physically healthy ; many of them even appear happy. So long as they remain in the institution there is no obvious ground for concern, yet when they leave they go to pieces, and it is evident that their adjustment had a hollow quality and was not based on a real growth of personality. (Goldfarb [66] has made a detailed study of this in children of about three years of age.) Satisfaction is also expressed on occasion that a child has completely forgotten his mother. Not only is this usually not true, as he shows when he cries for her when in distress, but when it is true it is very serious, for it is on the steady growth and expansion of this relationship that his future mental health depends.

Naturally the particular sequences or mixtures of reactions shown by different children will vary, and will depend greatly on the conditions in which they are living. The advent of a mother-substitute may change a group of apathetic or amiably undiscriminating children into possessive and tempestuous little savages. On the introduction of a substitute mother, Burlingham & Freud [39] report :

" Children, who have shown themselves adaptable and accommodating under group conditions, suddenly become insufferably demanding and unreasonable. Their jealousy and, above all, their possessiveness of the beloved grown-up may be boundless. It easily becomes compulsive where the mother-relationship is no new experience but where separation from a real mother or (and) a former foster-mother has occurred before. The child is all the more clinging, the more it has an inner conviction that separation will repeat itself. Children become disturbed in their play activities when they watch anxiously whether their ' own ' nurse leaves the room on an errand or for her off-hour or whether she has any intimate dealings with children outside her family. Tony, three and one-half, for instance, would not allow Sister Mary to use ' his ' hand for handling other children. Jim, two to three, would burst into tears whenever his ' own ' nurse left the room. Shirley, four years, would become intensely depressed and disturbed when ' her ' Marion was absent for some reason, etc. It is true that all these children had had to cope with a series of traumatic separations in their lives."

Many a mother whose young child has been away from her for a few weeks or months can confirm and amplify such observations. Sometimes on reunion the child is emotionally frozen, unable to express his feelings, sometimes unable even to speak. Then, in a torrent, his feelings thaw. Tearful sobs are succeeded (in those able to speak) by an accusatory " Why did you leave me, Mummy ? " Thenceforward for many weeks or months he never allows his mother out of his sight, he is babyish, anxious, and easily angered. Wisely handled, these troubles may gradually fade away, though once again the real possibility of unseen psychic scars must not be forgotten which may be reactivated and give rise to neurosis in later life. That this is a real danger is made clear by Robertson & Bowlby, who have observed acute phobic responses in children, who have apparently recovered emotional equilibrium, when confronted by someone whom they associate with the separation experience (unpublished observation). If the regressive anxious behaviour on return home is unsympathetically handled, vicious circles in the child's relation to his mother develop, bad behaviour being met by rebuffs and punishments, rebuffs and punishments calling forth more babyishness, more demands, more tempers. In this way develops the unstable neurotic personality, unable to come to terms with himself or the world, unable especially to make loving and loyal relationships with other people.

Disturbing though such a sequence of events may be, it is almost certainly less sinister than the case of the child who responds either by withdrawal or by an undiscriminating and shallow friendliness. These responses, which are probably the result of frequent separations or of prolonged separation occurring before about $2\frac{1}{2}$ years of age and without a substitute figure being available, are the precursors of the grave personality disturbances, commonly called psychopathic, which will be described fully in the next chapter.

At what age, it may be asked, does the child cease to be vulnerable to a lack of maternal care ? No doubt vulnerability diminishes slowly and, perhaps, asymptotically. All who have studied the matter would agree that vulnerability between three and five is still serious, though much less so than earlier. During this period children no longer live exclusively in the present and can consequently conceive dimly of a time when their mothers will return, which is beyond the capacity of most children younger than three. Furthermore, the ability to talk permits of simple explanations, and the child will take more readily to understanding substitutes. During this age-period, therefore, it may be said that wise and insightful management can go far to mitigate ill-effects, though in its absence very serious reactions, comparable to those of the child between one and three, are not uncommon.

After the age of five vulnerability diminishes still further, though there can be no reasonable doubt that a fair proportion of children between the ages of five and seven or eight are unable to adjust satisfactorily to separations, especially if they are sudden and there has been no preparation. A vivid and distressing picture has been given,[88] by the now grown-up patient, of what it felt like for a boy of six to be incarcerated in hospital for three years. He describes " the desperate homesickness and misery of the early weeks [which] gave way to indifference and boredom during the subsequent months ". He describes how he made a passionate attachment to the matron which compensated for the loss of home, but how, on returning, he felt out of place and an intruder. " In the end, this barrenness led me away from home again ... but no second mother-figure came my way, and indeed I was not then capable of creating stable relationships ... my responses were exaggerated, often uncalled for, and I became extremely moody and depressed ... I also became aggressive." Finally, after describing how he had, in later years, gained some understanding of himself, he writes : " I still have aggressions ... They take the unfortunate form of making me excessively intolerant to my own faults in other people, and are therefore a menace to my relationship with my own children." The impairment of the capacity for successful parenthood is perhaps the most damaging of all the effects of deprivation, a point emphasized in Part II of this report.

Confirmation of this picture is given by Edelston [52] and by more than one study of English children evacuated from the cities during the late war. Edelston gives valuable case-histories of some dozens of children whose neurotic symptoms had either developed or been made worse by separation from the mother, most of the separation experiences being in hospital. Although he does not make a systematic analysis of the age at which the children experienced hospitalization, a reading of his cases makes it plain that, although in about half of them it was during the first three years, in the other half the traumatic experience occurred between about three and eight years. In many of the latter the children could describe clearly how they had felt in hospital, common anxieties being the beliefs either that they would not return home or that they were being sent away for being naughty. Thus a boy of $7\frac{1}{2}$ who had been three times in hospital or convalescent-home since the age of $3\frac{1}{2}$ remarked : " I thought I was never coming home again because I was only six years old. I heard my sister say they were going to dump me and that I'd never come home again." Another child, a girl of $6\frac{3}{4}$, when being sent to fever hospital in her third year had cried : " I will be a good girl—don't send me." On returning home she was very quiet and sat scared in a corner much of the time. Though she never talked of this experience, she would play elaborate hospital games with her dolls in which sending them away to hospital was a punishment for naughtiness.

In the surveys of evacuated children between the ages of 5 and 16 undertaken during the late war, there were a sufficient number of reports of an adverse response to confirm this account and to make it clear that children of this age are not yet emotionally self-supporting. Teachers reported that homesickness was prevalent and power of concentration on schoolwork declined. Bedwetting increased.[81] Burt [42] estimated the overall frequency of nervous symptoms and delinquency to have increased from 17% to 25% of the school population. Though in many cases these responses were transitory and of no serious import, in others the problems persisted on return home. This is mentioned in the British Ministry of Health's survey,[76] and by Carey-Trefzer,[43] whose detailed clinical work is discussed later.

While there is reason to believe that all children under three and a very large proportion between three and five suffer through deprivation, in the case of those between five and eight it is probably only a minority and the question arises—why some and not others ? Contrary to what obtains in the younger age-groups, for children of this age the better their relation to their mothers the better can they tolerate separation. A happy child, secure in his mother's love, is not made pathologically anxious ; the insecure child, apprehensive of his mother's good feelings towards him, may easily misinterpret events. These misinterpretations, moreover, may smoulder on unknown to anyone, almost unknown to the child himself. The belief that he has been sent away for naughtiness leads to anxiety and hatred, and these in turn to a vicious circle in his relations to his parents. Thus children aged five or eight, who are already prone to emotional troubles, can easily be made far worse by a separation experience, whereas secure children of the same age may come through almost unscathed. Even so, for both groups much will depend on how the child is prepared for the situation, how he is treated during it, and how his mother handles him on his return. Both Edelston [52] and Isaacs [82] have discussed these aspects.

Finally, mention may be made of two very recent studies which, like those of Bakwin, stem from a paediatric and not a psychiatric tradition. These are studies of the growth curves of schoolchildren as measured by the Wetzel Grid,[147] which is a useful device for taking simultaneous account of height and weight changes and also allows for constitutional differences in physique. Neither study gives statistical details, but the two are in close agreement and confirm one another to some degree. Binning,[19] after studying 800 Canadian schoolchildren, reports that changes in the speed of growth are frequently emotional in origin and may take the form either of an acceleration or a lag.

" We found that events in the child's life that caused separation from one or both parents—death, divorce, enlistment of a parent—and a mental environment which gave the child a feeling that normal love and affection was lacking, did far more to damage growth than did disease, was more serious than all other factors combined in this day of full employment and family allowances."

He also reports that, as growth lag increased, there was increasing danger of either psychosomatic symptoms or behaviour difficulties developing. Fried & Mayer [56] found similar growth disturbances. They studied boys and girls between the ages of about 6 and 13 years admitted to an institution (Cottage Home) on account of personality disturbances following divorce, rejection, or death of parents, and concluded that " socio-emotional disturbance tends to affect physical growth adversely, and that growth failure so caused is much more frequent and more extensive than is generally recognized ". They proceed :

" there is, in most of our children with growth failure, a very striking and close parallelism between this physical affliction and socio-emotional adjustment. Onset and recovery in the one is accompanied quite simultaneously by corresponding progress in the other. The great majority of children who show either, show both, and the disturbances are roughly equal, that is, milder and severer forms of physical growth failure are associated with corresponding degrees of emotional trouble."

Binning [20] reports another parallel between physical and mental development, this time between physical growth and intelligence.

" Similarly when the Wetzel Grid shows lag in physical growth, mental growth as shown by Stanford-Binet tests also lags. Indeed when plotting Wetzel grids on children where two intelligence tests have been done, it is possible to predict with uncanny accuracy from the physical growth record just how much reduction of intelligence has taken place in a given time."

These results, if confirmed, are clearly of the greatest interest, opening up new possibilities of research into the interrelation of psyche and soma and providing the clinician with a simple and reliable tool. It must be emphasized, however, that, in contrast to other findings reported here, these conclusions must for the present be regarded as tentative.

CHAPTER 3

REVIEW OF EVIDENCE ON EFFECTS OF DEPRIVATION
II : RETROSPECTIVE AND FOLLOW-UP STUDIES

Retrospective Studies

Some of the immediately adverse effects of deprivation on young children and some of the short-term after-effects have now been discussed and note taken that those without training in mental health are apt either to deny the existence of such responses or to waive them aside as of no consequence. In this chapter, the tremendous weight of evidence will be reviewed which makes it clear that those who view these responses with concern, so far from crying wolf, are calling attention to matters of grave medical and social significance.

During the late 1930s, at least six independent workers were struck by the frequency with which children who committed numerous delinquencies, who seemed to have no feelings for anyone and were very difficult to treat, were found to have had grossly disturbed relationships with their mothers in their early years. Persistent stealing, violence, egotism, and sexual misdemeanours were among their less pleasant characteristics. Since 1937 there have been many papers on the subject, several of which originated independently and some of which were completed in ignorance of the work of others. The unanimity of their conclusions stamps their findings as authentic.

One of the first cases was recorded by Levy [91] and still stands as typical :

" My first example is an eight-year-old girl who was adopted a year and a half before referral. After an illegitimate birth, the child was shifted about from one relative to another, finally brought to a child placing agency, and then placed in a foster-home for two months before she came to the referring foster parents. The complaints were lying and stealing. The parents described the child's reaction to the adoption as very casual. When they brought her home and showed her the room she was to have all for herself, and took her on a tour of the house and grounds, she showed apparently no emotional response. Yet she appeared very vivacious and ' affectionate on the surface '. After a few weeks of experience with her, the mother complained to the husband that the child did not seem able to show any affection. The child, to use the mother's words, ' would kiss you but it would mean nothing '. The husband told his wife that she was expecting too much, that she should give the child a chance to get adapted to the situation. The mother was somewhat mollified by these remarks, but still insisted that something was wrong. The father said he saw nothing wrong with the child. In a few months, however, he made the same complaint. By this time, also, it was noted that the child was deceitful and evasive. All methods of correction were of no avail. . . The school teacher complained of her general inattention and her lack of pride in the way her things looked. However, she did well in her school subjects, in keeping with her good intelligence. She also made friends with children, though none of these were close friendships. After a contact of a year and a half with the patient the father said, ' You just can't get to her ', and the mother remarked, ' I have no more idea to-day what's going on in that child's mind than I knew the day she came. You can't get under her skin. She never tells what she's thinking or what she feels. She chatters but it's all surface'."

Here, in brief, are many of the typical features :

superficial relationships ;
no real feeling—no capacity to care for people or to make true friends ;
an inaccessibility, exasperating to those trying to help ;
no emotional response to situations where it is normal—a curious lack of concern ;
deceit and evasion, often pointless ;
stealing ;
lack of concentration at school.

The only atypical item in this case is the child's good schoolwork since more often than not this is seriously impaired.

In the same year as Levy's paper (1937) and in the years following, papers were published in the USA by Powdermaker et al. (1937), Lowrey (1940), Bender (1941, 1946, and 1947), and Goldfarb (9 papers 1943-1949), and in Britain by Bowlby (1940 and 1944). With monotonous regularity each put his finger on the child's inability to make relationships as being the central feature from which all the other disturbances sprang, and on the history of institutionalization or, as in the case quoted, of the child's being shifted about from one foster-mother to another as being its cause. So similar are the observations and the conclusions—even the very words— that each might have written the others' papers :

" These case illustrations are given as examples of emotional pathology caused by primary affect hunger of a severe degree. The symptom complaints are of various types. They include, frequently, aggressive and sexual behaviour in early life, stealing, lying, often of the fantastic type, and, essentially, complaints variously expressed, that indicate some lack of emotional response in the child. It is this lack of emotional response, this shallowness of affect, that explains the difficulty in modifying behaviour " (Levy [91]).

" Early in the work a third group of girls was recognized who were asocial but not obviously neurotic, and with whom no treatment methods seemed of any avail. Later it became clear that the feature common to them was an inability to make a real transference to any member of the staff. There might seem to be a good contact but it invariably proved to be superficial. . . There might be protestations of interest and a boisterous show of affection, but there was little or no evidence of any real attachment having been made. In going over their previous history, this same feature was outstanding. . . [These girls] have apparently had no opportunity to have a libidinal relationship in early childhood [and] seem to have little or no capacity to enter into an emotional relation with another person or with a group " (Powdermaker et al.[117]).

" All the children [28 in number] present certain common symptoms of inadequate personality development, chiefly related to an inability to give or receive affection ;

in other words, inability to relate the self to others—the isolation factor. . . The conclusion seems inescapable that infants reared in institutions undergo an isolation type
of experience, with a resulting isolation type of personality " (Lowrey [96]).

" Two special problems were referred to the ward from two child-placing agencies.
One came from an agency [in which] there is a feeling that no attachment should be allowed
to develop between the child and the boarding home so that by the time the child is
five years old, he has no attachment to anybody and no pattern of behaviour. . . Another
special group consisted of children placed in infancy [who] are given the best pediatric
care. . . but have been deprived of social contacts and play materials. . . These
children are unable to accept love, because of their severe deprivation in the first three
years. . . They have no play pattern, cannot enter into group play but abuse other
children. . . They are hyperkinetic and distractible ; they are completely confused
about human relationships. . . This type of child does not respond to the nursery group
and continues overactive, aggressive and asocial " (Bender & Yarnell [15]).

" Imperviousness and a limited capacity for affective relationships " characterize
children who have spent their early years in an institution. " Can it be that the absence
of affective relationship in infancy made it difficult or even unnecessary for the institution
children to participate later in positive emotional relationships. . . ? " (Goldfarb [62]).

Meanwhile, insulated from communication with these workers by the
Atlantic Ocean, Bowlby [25] was making identical observations in London :

" Prolonged breaks [in the mother-child relationship] during the first three years
of life leave a characteristic impression on the child's personality. Clinically such children
appear emotionally withdrawn and isolated. They fail to develop libidinal ties with other
children or with adults and consequently have no friendships worth the name. It is
true that they are sometimes sociable in a superficial sense, but if this is scrutinized we
find that there are no feelings, no roots in these relationships. This, I think, more than
anything else, is the cause of their hard-boiledness. Parents and school-teachers complain
that nothing you say or do has any effect on the child. If you thrash him he cries for
a bit, but there is no emotional response to being out of favour, such as is normal to the
ordinary child. It appears to be of no essential consequence to these lost souls whether
they are in favour or not. Since they are unable to make genuine emotional relations,
the condition of a relationship at a given moment lacks all significance for them . . .
During the last few years I have seen some sixteen cases of this affectionless type of
persistent pilferer and in only two was a prolonged break absent. In all the others gross
breaches of the mother-child relation had occurred during the first three years, and the
child had become a persistent pilferer."

Since these early communications there have been three major publications—a systematic clinical and statistical study by Bowlby,[26, 27] a review
by Bender [14] based on some hundreds of cases seen in the previous ten
years, and a series of papers describing most carefully planned and executed
research by Goldfarb.[60-68] Both Bender's and Bowlby's studies are retrospective in the sense that, as clinicians, they were called upon to examine
and treat children showing neurotic symptoms and disturbances of behaviour
and, by working back into the children's histories, unearthed the common
factor of deprivation of maternal care—caused either by their being in
institutions, or being posted, like parcels, from one mother-figure to
another. The objection to these retrospective studies is, of course, that they
are concerned only with children who have developed adversely, and fail
to take account of those who may have had the same experience but

have developed normally. This shortcoming, however, is made good in ample fashion by Goldfarb.

Bender's conclusions [14] are based on the 5% to 10% of the 5,000 children whom she had under her care in Bellevue Hospital from 1935-1944 and who showed the characteristics already described. She gives a full clinical description of the syndrome, which she terms 'psychopathic behaviour disorder of childhood'.

" There is an inability to love or feel guilty. There is no conscience. The unconscious fantasy material is shallow and shows only a tendency to react to immediate impulses or experiences, although there often are abortive efforts to experience an awareness of the ego or to identify the personality. Their inability to enter into any relationship makes therapy or even education impossible. There is an inability to conceptualize, particularly significant in regard to time. They have no concept of time, so that they cannot recall past experience and cannot benefit from past experience or be motivated to future goals. This lack of time concept is a striking feature in the defective organization of the personality structure . . . "

TABLE IV. INCIDENCE OF SEPARATION AND AFFECTIONLESS CHARACTER IN A GROUP OF THIEVES AND A CONTROL GROUP OF EMOTIONALLY DISTURBED CHILDREN WHO DID NOT STEAL (BOWLBY)

	Thieves			Controls
	affectionless	others	all	
Separation	12	5	17	2
No separation	2	25	27	42
Totals	14	30	44	44

Note : Both for the affectionless thieves versus the others, and for all the thieves versus controls, P is less than .01, which means that there is less than one chance in a hundred that the result is due to chance.

Bender also reports a follow-up study of ten children referred to in her 1941 paper who were seen five years later. This showed that " all remained infantile, unhappy and affectless and unable to adjust to children in the schoolroom or other group situation."

Bowlby,[26, 27] besides giving fairly full case-histories, in some of which the child's response to the traumatic experience can be traced, lays especial emphasis on the tendency of these children to steal. Dividing all the cases he had seen at a child-guidance clinic into those who had been reported as stealing and those who had not, he compares a group of 44 thieves with a control group, similar in number, age, and sex, who although emotionally disturbed did not steal. The thieves were distinguished from the controls in two main ways. First, there were among them 14 children whom Bowlby describes as ' affectionless characters ', while there were none in the control group. Secondly, 17 of the thieves had suffered complete and prolonged separation (six months or more) from their mothers or established foster-mothers during their first five years of life ; only 2 of the controls had suffered similar separations. Neither of these differences can be accounted for by chance. Two further points of great importance were that there was a high and statistically significant degree of overlap between the ' affectionless characters ' and those with a history of separation, and that the affectionless children were far more delinquent than any of the others. Bowlby's results can be tabulated as in table IV.

The overwhelmingly high incidence of separation among the affectionless thieves stands out. When this is contrasted with the incidence of a bad heredity, there can be no doubting that for the affectionless thief nurture rather than nature is the pathogenic agent (see table V).

TABLE V. INCIDENCE OF ADVERSE GENETIC FACTORS IN A GROUP OF THIEVES AND A CONTROL GROUP OF EMOTIONALLY DISTURBED CHILDREN WHO DID NOT STEAL (BOWLBY)

	Thieves			Controls
	affectionless	others	all	
Bad heredity	3	16	19	18
Heredity not bad	11	14	25	26
Totals	14	30	44	44

In assessing heredity the presence of neurosis, psychosis, or serious psychopathy in parents or grandparents is taken as the criterion. Evidence is admittedly most imperfect but equally so for the controls as for the thieves. Moreover, the internal clinical evidence in several cases of affectionless character makes it fairly clear that it was the experience of prolonged separation from the mother which was to blame. After reviewing evidence from the work of Burt,[41] Glueck & Glueck,[59] and others which is implicitly confirmatory, Bowlby concludes :

" on the basis of this varied evidence it appears that there is a very strong case indeed for believing that prolonged separation of a child from his mother (or mother substitute) during the first five years of life stands foremost among the causes of delinquent character development ".

Among the cases presented by Bowlby is one of a boy who was believed to have had a good relation to his mother until the age of 18 months but who was then in hospital for nine months, during which time visiting by his parents was forbidden. Others of Bowlby's cases suggest that hospitalization and changes of mother-figure as late as the fourth year can have very destructive effects.

Both Bender and Bowlby thus independently advance the hypothesis that there is a specific connexion between prolonged deprivation in the early years and the development of an affectionless psychopathic character given to persistent delinquent conduct and extremely difficult to treat.

Of the many other retrospective studies which touch on this problem, though without making this precise connexion, mention has already been made of that by Edelston.[52] Four others will be briefly described. Carey-Trefzer,[43] examining the records of some 200 children under the age of 12 seen at a child-guidance clinic in London during the years 1942-1946 and whose troubles seemed to have been caused or aggravated by the war, found that in 32.5% of the cases the trouble had been caused by evacuation. She proceeds :

"The clinical study has revealed without doubt that evacuation has played a major role both in aggravating neurotic symptoms and in creating deep and persisting disturbances . . . Almost all the 'difficult' and long treatment cases are evacuation cases. "

This is in contrast, it must be emphasized, to experience of bombing. No less than two-thirds of the children who presented problems after evacuation had been under the age of five when first evacuated. Since the number of young children evacuated in proportion to older ones was small, the figures make clear the extent to which it is especially the young child who is damaged by experiences of this kind.

A review of the total population of the Hawthorne-Cedar Knolls School, near New York, was carried out in April 1950.[83] There were then in residence 137 boys and 62 girls, all but a few of whom were between 13 and 17 years of age. The school specializes in cases presenting grave psychiatric disorders, the principal diagnoses being psychoneurosis 28%, schizophrenia 21%, character neurosis 19%, primary behaviour disorder 13%, and psychopathic personality 10%. The problems comprised truancy and running away, stealing, sexual offences, conflicts with parents, and other aggressive behaviour. Of these children, 14% had been in institutions and 24% in foster-homes before the age of 4. Although these figures cannot be summed, since some children were in both an institution and a foster-home before this age, the degree of disruption of parent-child relations for the whole group is shown by only 25% of them having been brought up by both parents. There are few establishments catering for this type of case which would not show similar figures.

Among studies of adult patients, which have led their authors to the conclusion that love deprivation is the cause of the psychiatric condition, may be mentioned those by Fitzgerald[55] of hysterical patients and Kemp[89] of prostitutes. Fitzgerald advances the view that

"regardless of the nature of an individual's inborn tendencies, he will not develop hysteria unless he is subjected during childhood to situations causing him to crave affection ".

Among such situations he lists death of a parent and separation of child from parents. Kemp, who collected information on 530 prostitutes in Copenhagen, found that one-third of them had not been brought up at home but had spent their childhood under troubled and shifting conditions :

"3% were brought up by close relations, 3% were boarded out or sent to a home, 27% were raised under combined conditions, partly in homes or almshouses, partly in institutions for the feeble-minded or epileptics, partly at home or with relatives" (page 85).

Sometimes they had three or four different foster-homes during the course of their childhood. 17% of the total were illegitimate.

Further evidence tracing delinquency, promiscuity, neurosis, and even psychosis to deprivation, bereavement, and broken homes is given in Appendix 1.[f]

Follow-up Studies

All the inquiries so far described have the shortcomings inherent in the retrospective method ; the follow-up studies of Goldfarb and others are therefore of especial value since they take a group of children institutionalized in infancy and seek to determine how they have developed.

The outstanding quality of Goldfarb's work derives from its having been scientifically planned from the beginning to test the hypothesis that the experience of living in the highly impersonal surroundings of an institution nursery in the first two or three years of life has an adverse effect on personality development. With this end in view he selected his samples so that, so far as is possible, they were similar in heredity, and thereby controlled a variable which has been the bugbear of most other investigations. Altogether he has done three main studies.[60, 62, 66] In each he has compared the mental development of children, brought up until the age of about three in an institution and then placed in foster-homes, with others who had gone straight from their mothers to foster-homes in which they had remained. In both samples the children had been handed over by their mothers in infancy, usually within the first nine months of life. The sample most thoroughly studied consisted of 15 pairs of children who, at the time of the examination, ranged in age from 10 to 14 years.[62] One set of 15 was in the institution from about 6 months of age to $3\frac{1}{2}$ years, the other set had not had this experience. Conditions in the institution conformed to the highest standards of physical hygiene but lacked the elementary essentials of mental hygiene :

"Babies below the age of nine months were each kept in their own little cubicles to prevent the spread of epidemic infection. Their only contacts with adults occurred during these few hurried moments when they were dressed, changed or fed by nurses."

Later they were members of a group of 15 or 20 under the supervision of one nurse, who had neither the training nor the time to offer them love or attention. As a result they lived in " almost complete social isolation during that first year of life " and their experience in the succeeding two years was only slightly richer. Goldfarb has gone to great pains to ensure that the foster-homes of the two groups are similar in respect of all observable criteria and demonstrates further that, in respect of the mother's occupational, educational, and mental status, the institution group was slightly superior to the controls. Any differences in the mental states of the two groups of children are, therefore, virtually certain to be the result of their differing experiences in infancy.

The two groups of children were studied by a great variety of tests and rating scales and all differences checked for the possible influence of chance. A few of the very numerous and striking differences are listed in tables VI and VII.

TABLE VI. DIFFERENCES BETWEEN CHILDREN WHO HAD SPENT THEIR FIRST THREE YEARS IN AN INSTITUTION AND CONTROLS WHO HAD NOT (GOLDFARB)

Function tested or rated	Test or rating method	Result expressed as	Results	
			institution group	control group
Intelligence	Wechsler	mean IQ	72.4	95.4
Ability to conceptualize . . .	Weigl Vigotsky	mean score mean score	2.4 0.5	6.8 4.7
Reading	standard tests	mean score	5.1	6.8
Arithmetic	standard tests	mean score	4.7	6.7
Social maturity . . .	Vineland Scale completed by case-workers	mean social quotient	79.0	98.8
Ability to keep rules.	frustration experiment	number of children	3	12
Guilt on breaking rules		number of children	2	11
Capacity for relationships . . .	case-worker's assessment	number of children able to make normal relationships	2	15
Speech		number of children up to average	3	14
Number of children (total)			15	15

Note : In the case of all differences shown, P is less than .01.

The number and consistency of these differences is truly remarkable. The disability in the cognitive field is striking and confirmed by several other tests. It is obviously connected with the lowered developmental and intelligence levels observed by those who have made direct studies, and makes it clear that, in some cases at least, the retardation of the institutionalized infant or toddler persists. Goldfarb's discoveries regarding the institution child's inability to conceptualize are particularly valuable

TABLE VII. INCIDENCE OF PROBLEMS IN CHILDREN WHO HAD SPENT THEIR FIRST THREE YEARS IN AN INSTITUTION AND CONTROLS WHO HAD NOT (GOLDFARB)

Problem	Rated by	Result expressed as	Results	
			institution group	control group
Unpopular with other children	case-worker	number of children showing problem	6	1
Craving affection	''	'' ''	9	2
Fearful	''	'' ''	8	1
Restless, hyperactive . . .	''	''	9	1
Inability to concentrate . . .	''	'' ''	10	0
Poor school achievement . .	''	'' ''	15	1
Number of children (total)			15	15

Note : In all cases but the first, P is less than .01. In the first case, it lies between .05 and .02.

as giving a clue to some of the psychological processes underlying the personality disturbances, a point discussed later. Another point which emerges from Goldfarb's work is the persistence of the speech disabilities, noted by so many of the direct observers. In this, he confirms the earlier observations of Lowrey.[96]

Goldfarb's findings [64] regarding the responses to the Rorschach test given by the two groups are set out in Appendix 2.[g] Among the many statistically significant differences are those related to the institution children's inability to conceptualize, their tendency to arbitrary responses, confabulations, lack of control over emotional responses, and diminished drive toward social conformity. Some of these were also found by Loosli-Usteri [94] in her Rorschach study of institution children in Geneva, the findings of which confirm the general conclusion that institution children are psychiatrically disturbed. An outline of this study is given in the same appendix.

Most of Goldfarb's findings in regard to personality disturbances are in line with those of Bender and Bowlby. There are, however, certain differences which are not always easy to interpret (especially in the absence of case-histories, an omission which it is to be hoped Goldfarb will one day make good). The contrast between Goldfarb's finding that institution children " crave affection " and Bowlby's observation of their being " affectionless " is probably more apparent than real. Many affectionless characters crave affection, but nonetheless have a complete inability either to accept or reciprocate it. The poor capacity of all but two of Goldfarb's children for making relationships is clearly confirmatory of all other work.

---

g See page 166.

The fact that only one of this sample of Goldfarb's institution children stole and none truanted is, however, surprising in view of Bowlby's findings. The difference is probably valid and needs explanation. It will be discussed in the next chapter.

The tenor of Goldfarb's summary of his findings in regard to personality disturbances will by now be familiar to the reader :

" Briefly, the institution children present a history of aggressive, distractible, uncontrolled behaviour. Normal patterns of anxiety and self-inhibition are not developed. Human identifications are limited, and relationships are weak and easily broken . . . [68]

" Finally, the fact that the personality distortions caused by early deprivation are not overcome by later community and family experience must be stressed. There is a continuity of essential traits as late as adolescence. If anything, there is a growing inaccessibility to change." [62]

One shortcoming in his discussion should, however, be noted—namely, his tendency to imply that all institutions and their products are the same. This will be referred to later. None the less, for skilful planning and care of execution, Goldfarb's work ranks high ; not until a comparable piece of work has been done with different results can there be reason to doubt his findings.

There are, moreover, several other follow-up studies which, though far less thorough, are in some degree confirmatory. Lowrey,[96] in the paper already quoted, studied a sample of children comprising, among others, 22 unselected cases who with one exception had been admitted to an institution before their first birthday and had remained there until they were three or four, when they were transferred to another agency for fostering. Lowrey examined them when they were five years of age or older. All of them showed severe personality disturbances centering on an inability to give or receive affection. Symptoms, each of which occurred in half or more of them, included aggressiveness, negativism, selfishness, excessive crying, food difficulties, speech defects, and enuresis. Other difficulties only a little less frequent included over-activity, fears, and soiling.

While both Goldfarb and Lowrey report 100% of children institutionalized in their early years to have developed very adversely, the studies of Theis [139] and of Beres & Obers [16] show that many such children achieve a tolerable degree of social adaptation when adult. Though this finding is in accordance with the expectations of the man in the street, it would be a mistake to build too much on it since it is known that very many people who are psychiatrically disturbed are able to make a tolerable external adjustment for long periods. Moreover, both studies demonstrate a high incidence of overt disorder which the authors regard as confirming the pathogenicity of institutional conditions for young children.

As long ago as 1924, Theis [139] undertook a comprehensive study of the social adjustment as adults of 910 people who had been placed in foster-homes as children. In clinical and statistical care it remains in the first rank, and being a purely social study cannot be accused of psychiatric bias. A particularly interesting comparison is made between 95 children who had spent five years or more of their childhood in institutions and 84 who had spent the same years at home (in 80% of cases in bad homes). Not only had all the children of both groups, later, been placed in foster-homes of similar quality and at similar ages, but so far as could be determined the heredity of the two groups was similar. The results, which are given in table VIII, show that those brought up in an institution adjusted significantly less well than those who had remained during their first five years in their own homes. Since heredity is, so far as possible, held constant for these two groups, the difference cannot be explained in this way. Theis, indeed, goes into the evidence regarding heredity in fairly considerable detail for her whole sample and presents a table showing that the percentages of success among the offspring of good and of psychopathic parents do not differ significantly (see table XVII, page 122). The fact that no less than one-third of the institution children turned out to be ' socially incapable ', of which nearly half were troublesome and delinquent, is to be noted.

TABLE VIII. COMPARISON OF SOCIAL ADJUSTMENT OF CHILDREN WHO HAD SPENT FIVE YEARS OR MORE IN AN INSTITUTION AND THOSE WHO HAD HAD NO INSTITUTIONAL CARE (THEIS)

	Early childhood	
	in institution	not in institution
	%	%
Socially capable	65.5	82
Socially incapable		
Harmless	19	11
Harmful	15.5	7
On trial or in institution		
	100	100
Number of children	95	84

Note : P lies between .02 and .01.

It will be remarked, however, that, despite the institutional experience in the early years, two-thirds turned out ' socially capable '. So far as it goes this is satisfactory, but, as no psychiatric examination was carried out, neurotic and psychosomatic troubles not leading to social incompetence were not recorded. It is virtually certain that the incidence of psychiatric disturbance was much above the 34.5% of overt social incapacity.

Beres & Obers[16] have recently reported on a group of 38 subjects, aged between 16 and 28 (average 20) years, who had been institutionalized during their first three or four years of life. It is of interest as being the oldest age-group of its kind studied psychiatrically, but it has the very serious defect of not being a random sample : they were all cases requiring additional care and so may be supposed to be more heavily loaded in a pathological direction than a truly representative group. Of the 38, 4 were schizophrenic and 22 suffered from severe character disorders, 7 being affectionless psychopaths. A further 7 are stated to have made a satisfactory adjustment, though from the information given this would appear to have been precarious in some of them, and none had demonstrated his capacity to make a successful marriage partner or parent. What the study brings out clearly is that different children have very different experiences in institutions and respond in many different ways. The authors emphasize especially that not all children who spend their early years in an institution develop into affectionless psychopaths and that those who do not do so can often be greatly helped in later life. They make it clear, however, that institutionalization in early life is usually very injurious to personality growth.

TABLE IX. DISTRIBUTION OF SOCIAL MATURITY SCORES :
(a) BY EXPERIENCE (b) BY HEREDITY (BODMAN)

	Number of children	Mean score
(a) Sample divided by experience		
Institution experience	51	92.9
Family experience	52	106.5
(b) Sample divided by heredity		
Adverse factors in heredity.	28	91.6
No adverse factors in heredity	63	105.0

So far all the evidence has pointed in but one direction. It is now time to consider the three studies which present evidence which purports to call these conclusions in question. It may be said at once that none of them is of high scientific quality or bears comparison with the work either of Goldfarb or of Theis.

Orgel's paper [111] is a brief note commenting on that of Lowrey. He states that he has seen some 16 children, coming from the same institutions and having had the same experiences as Lowrey's sample, and that only two showed adverse features of personality. No details are given and there appears to have been no systematic clinical investigation.

Brown [33] compares a group of 100 boys aged 9 to 14 years living in an institution with another 100 of the same age living at home in bad surroundings, where broken homes and familial discords predominate. Using a personality inventory he shows that the two groups are similar in neuroticism. Not only is a personality inventory an unsatisfactory criterion, but no evidence is given regarding the age at which the children entered the institution.

The most recent of the three was carried out by Bodman and his associates [23, 24] in England. In it he compares the " social maturity " of two groups of 15-year-old children : 51 who had spent the previous three years or more in an institution and a comparable 52 who had lived at home. Using the Vineland Social Maturity Scale, he shows that, although the institution children have a lower score than the family children, when the cases are regrouped according to their heredity, an exactly similar difference is to be seen. The figures are set out in table IX.

No tests of significance appear to have been done.

On the basis of these figures, Bodman [23] concludes that

" such a finding certainly weakens the case of those protagonists who argue that any social or personal retardation is attributable exclusively or mainly to environmental influences "

and that it

" suggests that constitutional factors are at least as important as environmental factors in . . . social maturation ".

These conclusions are ill-judged and certainly cannot be sustained by the evidence presented. Very oddly, he has not undertaken a tabulation in which the effects of each variable is determined the other being held constant ; without this no conclusions are warranted. Apart from this, and the not very satisfactory nature of the Vineland Scale as a criterion, his sampling leaves much to be desired, inasmuch as some of the institution children did not enter until they were quite old, the average age of admission being four years ; while, even more serious, of the family children in the control group, no less than 22 had been evacuated from their homes during the war, the average length of time being one year and nine months. Work with so many shortcomings cannot be accepted as calling in question the almost unanimous findings of the workers already quoted.

There is one other group of data which is sometimes quoted as casting doubt on these findings—that from the Jewish communal settlements in Israel known as Kibbutz (plural, Kibbutzim). In these settlements, largely for ideological reasons, children are brought up by professional nurses in a ' Children's House '. Babies are reared in groups of 5 or 6, and are later merged at the age of three years into larger groups numbering 12 to 18. The emphasis is throughout on communal rather than family care. Is not this, it may be asked, a clear example that communal care can be made to work without damaging the children ? Before answering this question it is necessary to look more carefully at the conditions in which the children are raised. The following account is taken partly from the report of an

American psychiatric social worker, Alt, who recently visited Israel, and partly from a personal communication from the Lasker Mental Hygiene and Child Guidance Centre in Jerusalem. Both describe life in certain of the non-religious Kibbutzim. Alt [4] remarks :

" Separation is a relative concept and separation as it appears in the Kibbutz should not be thought of as identical with that of children who are brought up in foster-homes or institutions away from their parents . . . In the Kibbutz there is a great deal of opportunity for close relationship between child and parent."

Not only does the mother nurse the baby and feed him in the early months, but, to follow the Lasker Centre's description :

" once the suckling tie between mother and child is abandoned, the daily visit of the child to the room of the parents becomes the focus of family life for the child, and its importance is scrupulously respected. During these few hours the parents, or at least one of them, are more or less completely at the disposal of the children ; they play with them, talk to them, carry the babies about, take the toddlers for little walks, etc."

The time spent with the children " may amount to as much as two to three hours on working days and many more on the Sabbath " (Alt [4]).

Here, then, is no complete abandonment of parent-child relations. Though the amount of time parents spend with their young children is far less than in most other Western communities, the reports make it clear that the parents are extremely important people in the children's eyes, and the children in the parents'. It is interesting to note, too, that the trend is steadily towards parents taking more responsibility. Formerly parents had to visit the children in the Children's House—now the children come to the parents' room and the parents even prepare light meals for them ; feasts are now celebrated in the parents' room as well as communally in the Children's House ; mothers are asserting themselves and demanding to see more of their children.

Finally, it is by no means certain that the children do not suffer from this regime. While both observers report good and co-operative development in adolescence, the Lasker Centre think there are signs of " a somewhat higher level of insecurity among Kibbutz children than among others, at least until some point in the latency period ". They also point out that the strong morale and intimate group life of the Kibbutz are of great value to the older child and adolescent and that these may offset some of the unsettlement of earlier years.

From this brief account it is evident that there is no evidence here which can be held to invalidate the hypotheses. The conditions provide, of course, unusually rich opportunities for research in child development, and it is to be hoped these will not be missed.

Observations of War Orphans and Refugees

Evidence of the adverse effects on children of all ages of separation from their families was provided on a tragic scale during the second World War, when thousands of refugee children from occupied lands in Europe were cared for in Switzerland and elsewhere. Owing to the scale of the problem there was little time for systematic research, and in any case the children had been submitted to such diverse and often horrifying experiences that it would have been almost impossible to have isolated the effects of separation from those of other experiences. Brosse [31, 32] has summarized the findings of medical, educational, and relief workers and has emphasized that " while the reports tell of disturbances in character resulting from war, they show also the fundamental part played in their causation by rupture of the family tie ".[31] In the same volume, Meierhofer reports on experiences with refugee children at the Pestalozzi Village at Trogen, Switzerland :

" No doubt remains that a long period without individual attention and personal relationships leads to mental atrophy ; it slows down or arrests the development of the emotional life and thus in turn inhibits normal intellectual development. We have observed that acute psychical traumata, however serious, do not result in such deep injury as chronic deficiencies and prolonged spiritual solitude."

In 1944, Loosli-Usteri [95] undertook a small comparative study of 97 Jewish refugee children in homes in Switzerland and 173 Swiss children of about the same age (11 to 17 years). All the children were asked to write an essay on " What I think, what I wish and what I hope ". From a scrutiny of these essays she concluded that for the refugees " separation from their parents is evidently their most tragic experience ". In contrast, few of the Swiss children mention their parents, who were evidently felt to be a natural and inevitable part of life. Another great contrast was the refugee children's preoccupation with their suffering past, or frenzied and grandiose ideas regarding the future. The controls lived happily in the present, which for the refugees was either a vacuum or at best an unsatisfying transition. Deprived of all the things which had given life meaning, especially family and friends, they were possessed by a feeling of emptiness.

Szondi also studied refugee children in Switzerland and others in a concentration camp. He describes (personal communication) an ' uprooting syndrome ' comprising repression of the need to cling, which, however, manifests itself in symptoms such as bedwetting and stealing, an inability to make relations and a consequent loss of ability to form ideals, and an increase of aggression. He also remarks on the tendency towards an overactive hypomanic attitude. Intolerance of frustration, aggression, and the hypomanic response are mentioned by others with experience of such children.

In the Netherlands after the war, Tibout, de Leeuw, and Frijling studied some thousands of children whose parents had been deported in 1942 and 1943 and who had been cared for in foster-homes, often from earliest infancy. They report (verbal communications) that frequent changes of foster-home almost always had very adverse effects, leading the child to become withdrawn and apathetic. This was sometimes accompanied by a superficial sociability and, later, promiscuity. Some young children managed to weather a single change, but others could not stand even this and developed symptoms such as anxiety, depression, excessive clinging, and bed-wetting.   Many of the children were still emotionally disturbed when examined after the war and in need of treatment. It was noted that those who had had good family relationships before separation could usually be helped to an adjustment, but that those with a bad family background had a poor prognosis.

Finally may be noted an extensive psychological and statistical study undertaken in Spain following the civil war ; since it came to hand late and is presented in a language unfamiliar to the writer, it has been impossible to do it justice.   Piquer y Jover [114] and his associates report their findings on over 14,000 cases of neglected and delinquent children housed in the environs of Barcelona.   Once again there is confirmation of the decisive and adverse role in character development played by the break-up of the family, and the vital importance of family life for satisfactory social and moral development.   Particularly interesting is the confirmation of Goldfarb's findings regarding impaired cognitive development. The IQs of the neglected and delinquent children are 20 to 40 points below those of a control group.   Piquer y Jover believes the evidence demonstrates that this considerable reduction is the result of environmental rather than hereditary factors and suspects that lack of education is partly to blame for poor performances on tests such as the Stanford-Binet. Impairment of the capacity for abstract thought is also noted—the evidence, in the investigator's opinion, pointing to " the existence of a strong correlation between the development of the abstract mental faculties and the family and social life of the child ". He notes especially the following characteristics of the neglected and delinquent child :

" Feeble and difficult attention due to his great instability.
Very slight sense of objective realities, overflowing imagination and absolute lack of critical ability.
Incapacity for strict abstraction and logical reasoning . . .
Noteworthy backwardness in the development of language . . ." [h]

The similarity of these observations on war orphans and refugees to those on other deprived children will not fail to impress the reader.

---

[h] Quoted from the author's English abstract.

CHAPTER 4

INTERIM CONCLUSIONS

The evidence has been reviewed at some length because much of it is still little known and the issue of whether deprivation causes psychiatric disturbance is still discussed as though it were an open question. It is submitted that the evidence is now such that it leaves no room for doubt regarding the general proposition—that the prolonged deprivation of the young child of maternal care may have grave and far-reaching effects on his character and so on the whole of his future life. Although it is a proposition exactly similar in form to those regarding the evil after-effects of rubella in foetal life or deprivation of vitamin D in infancy, there is a curious resistance to accepting it. Indeed, there are still psychiatrists in all countries who challenge these conclusions, though it is to be remarked that few of them have had training in child psychiatry or experience of work in a child-guidance clinic. Their clinical work is confined to the examination of older patients of an age when it is difficult or impossible to obtain light on what really happened in their early years. Moreover, so embittered and distorted is the information patients commonly give about their childhood experiences that many psychiatrists and even psycho-analysts have regarded their stories as no more than fantasies and have wholly discounted the really adverse effects of an unhappy childhood. It is, of course, true that there are still far too few systematic studies and statistical comparisons in which proper control groups have been used. Relatively few studies taken by themselves are more than suggestive. But when all the evidence is fitted together it is seen to be remarkably consistent and this, taken with the considered opinions of experienced child-guidance workers in many different countries, leaves no doubt that the main proposition is true. Reluctance to accept it is, perhaps, because to do so would involve far-reaching changes in conceptions of human nature and in methods of caring for young children.

However that may be, although the main proposition may be regarded as established, knowledge of details remains deplorably small. It is as though it had been established that an absence of vitamin D caused rickets and that calcium was in some way involved, but as yet no quantitative measures were available and there was complete ignorance of the many interrelated associated factors. That deprivation can have bad consequences is known, but how much deprivation children of different ages can withstand has yet to be determined. The evidence available may now be summarized and such conclusions drawn as are permissible.

In the first place, there is abundant evidence that deprivation can have adverse effects on the development of children (a) during the period of separation, (b) during the period immediately after restoration to maternal care, and (c) permanently. The fact that some children seem to escape is of no consequence. The same is true of the consumption of tubercular-infected milk or exposure to the virus of infantile paralysis. In both these cases a sufficient proportion of children is so severely damaged that no one would dream of intentionally exposing a child to such hazards. Deprivation of maternal care in early childhood falls into the same category of dangers.

Most of the evidence in respect of long-term effects refers to the grave disturbances following severe deprivation ; it is easiest to work from these established connexions to those which are less well understood. The evidence suggests that three somewhat different experiences can each produce the affectionless and psychopathic character :

(a) lack of any opportunity for forming an attachment to a mother-figure during the first three years (Powdermaker, Bender, Lowrey, Goldfarb) ;

(b) deprivation for a limited period—at least three months and probably more than six—during the first three or four years (Bowlby, Spitz & Wolf) ;

(c) changes from one mother-figure to another during the same period (Levy, and others).

Though the gross results of these different experiences appear the same, it seems probable, both for theoretical and empirical reasons, that close study will reveal differences. For instance, it may well be that the discrepancy as regards stealing between the children studied by Bowlby [26, 27] and by Goldfarb [62] would be explained in this way. All of Goldfarb's cases had been institutionalized from soon after birth until they were three years old. None of Bowlby's had—they were all products of deprivation for a limited period, or of frequent changes. It may well be that their stealing was an attempt to secure love and gratification and so reinstate the love relationship which they had lost, whereas Goldfarb's cases, never having experienced anything of the kind, had nothing to reinstate. Certainly it would appear that the more complete the deprivation in the early years the more isolated and asocial the child, whereas the more that deprivation is interspersed with satisfaction, the more ambivalent and antisocial he becomes. Lowrey [96] may well be right in his belief that " children placed in institutions for short periods after the age of 2 do not develop this isolated type of personality or show the same behavior patterns " ; research at present in progress at the Tavistock Clinic tends to confirm this. Nevertheless, Carey-Trefzer [43] and Bowlby have each recorded a sufficient number of cases where the development of extremely antisocial characters, unable to make stable relations with anyone though not complete isolates, appeared to follow changes from one mother-figure to another during the fourth year, to make it clear that very evil results may follow even at this age. Naturally, the effects on personality development at any given age will depend on the exact nature of the experience to which the child is submitted, information about which is all too frequently missing from records. Indeed, one of the great shortcomings of present evidence is a lack of detail and precision on this point. It has already been remarked that implicit in Goldfarb's writings is the assumption that all infants and toddlers in institutions have similar experiences. Not only is it clear that they do not, but the more one studies all the data on the subject, the more he becomes convinced that the outcome is to a high degree dependent on the exact nature of the psychological experience. If further research is to be fruitful, it must pay minute attention not only to ages and periods of deprivation, but also to the quality of the child's relation to his mother before deprivation, his experiences with mother-substitutes, if any, during separation, and the reception he gets from his mother or foster-mother when at last he becomes settled again.

Though all workers on the subject are now agreed that the first year of life is of vital importance, there is at present some debate regarding the age at which deprivation has the most evil consequences. Bowlby, after reviewing his cases, noted that the separations which appeared pathogenic had all occurred after the age of six months and in a majority after that of 12 months, from which he was inclined to conclude that separations and deprivations in the first six months of life were less important for the child's welfare than later ones. This has also been the view of Anna Freud.[39] It has, however, been called in question explicitly by Spitz & Wolf (verbal communication), and implicitly by Klein,[86] whose data are of a very different kind, having been derived retrospectively from the psycho-analytic treatment of children and adults. Goldfarb also has attached especial importance to the first half-year, although, as is shown in Appendix 3,[i] his data do not really warrant the conclusion he draws from them. Nevertheless, this study of Goldfarb's,[65] in which he examines the social adjustment of adolescents in relation to the age at which they were admitted to the institution, points unmistakably to the special vulnerability of the child during the first year in comparison to later ones. Bender's references [13, 14] to children in whom the deprivation was limited to the first year and who none the less showed the classical retardation and personality distortion provide further evidence regarding the first year as a whole, though they do not contribute to the debate regarding the baby's vulnerability during the first half of it in particular.

For the present, therefore, it may be recorded that deprivation occurring in the second half of the first year of life is agreed by all students of the

---

i See page 169.

subject to be of great significance and that many believe this to be true also of deprivation occurring in the first half, especially from three to six months. The balance of opinion, indeed, is that considerable damage to mental health can be done by deprivation in these months, a view which is unquestionably supported by the direct observations, already described, of the immediately adverse effects of deprivation on babies of this age.

There is, however, a further point—the time limit within which the provision of mothering can make good some at least of the damage done by deprivation in these early months. The comparative success of many babies adopted between six and nine months who have spent their first half-year in conditions of deprivation makes it virtually certain that, for many babies at least, provided they receive good mothering in time, the effects of early damage can be greatly reduced. What Goldfarb's work demonstrates without any doubt is that such mothering is almost useless if delayed until after the age of $2\frac{1}{2}$ years. In actual fact this upper age limit for most babies is probably before 12 months. But the probable existence of a safety limit should not give rise to complacency : the fact that it may be possible to make good some of the damage done by deprivation in the early months is no excuse for permitting it to be inflicted in the first place.

So much for the fully fledged forms of psychopathic character and the experiences which produce them, a sequence of events now widely recognized by child psychiatrists. Ever since Levy's first paper, however, psychiatrists concerned with this problem have pointed to the existence of less gross conditions to which less severe deprivation could give rise and which are far and away more frequent. Not only are there the many partial and covert forms of psychopathic personality, including Fitzgerald's hysterics,[55] but many conditions of anxiety and depression almost certainly stem from deprivation experiences or have been exacerbated by them.

" Such examples ", Levy [91] writes, " are seen in those adults whose social life represents a series of relationships with older people, every one of whom is a substitute mother. They may be single or in combination, the point being simply that the patient must, throughout life, be in contact with a person from whom the same demands are made that were thwarted in the original experience with the mother. The life pattern then becomes dependent on maintaining such relationships. When one of them is broken there is a period of depression, or a feeling that ' something is terrifically lacking ', until another relationship is made. Another type of reaction is seen in the form chiefly of excessive demands made on the person who is selected to satisfy the privations of early life . . . The problem is always the same—excessive demands for food, for money, for privileges."

Not infrequently people with these troubles deny their existence by an excessive show of cheerfulness and activity—the hypomanic reaction. This is an attempt to convince themselves that God's in his heaven, all's right with the world, a state of affairs of which they are far from sure. Naturally the hypomanic method meets with some success but, based as it is on a denial,

is in constant danger of cracking and leaving its owner in a state of despair
Moreover, even while it succeeds, the press of activity and intolerance of
frustration are very trying to others, while, as Bowlby [26, 27] and Stott [137]
have shown, it not infrequently leads to delinquency.

Though such cases are sadly numerous, they are mercifully more acces-
sible to psycho-analytic therapy than the severe forms. On the immense
therapeutic task set by the fully fledged psychopaths all are agreed. Levy
described them in 1937 as having a poor prognosis, a view endorsed by
every worker since. Because of their almost complete inability to make
relationships, the psychotherapist is robbed of his principal therapeutic
tool : he should, of course, be skilled in the management of patients who
hate him ; he has yet to learn methods of affecting for the better patients
who have no feelings for him at all. The findings of Powdermaker et al.[117]
in this regard are especially clear. Working over a period of some six
years in a small home for delinquent girls between the ages of 12 and 16,
therapy was given to 80 of them. Half were successes and half failures.
Response to therapy was related neither to intelligence nor to heredity.
Its relationship to the girls' early family experiences, however, was striking.

TABLE X. RELATION OF THERAPEUTIC RESPONSE OF DELINQUENT GIRLS
TO THEIR EARLY FAMILY EXPERIENCES (POWDERMAKER ET AL.)

Early family experience	Effect of therapy	
	success	failure
No rejection and some constructive family tie present	25	0
Rejection by some member of the family but some constructive tie present also	12	10
Neurotic and ambivalent relationships	3	13
Complete rejection or no libidinal tie	0	17
Totals	40	40

Note : P is less than .01.

The failure in treatment of all those who had suffered rejection or had
never had a libidinal tie recalls Goldfarb's remark [67] that he has never
seen " even one example of significantly favorable response to treatment
by traditional methods of child psychiatry ". Bender [14] goes so far as to
say that " once the defect is created it cannot be corrected ", and recommends that methods of care should make no attempt to be therapeutic
or corrective but " should be protective and should aim to foster a dependent
relationship ". Others are more hopeful and believe that if the child is
permitted to regress to completely infantile modes of behaviour there is a
chance of his developing afresh along better lines. The work of Jonsson

at the Children's Village at Skå near Stockholm is an example of a European experiment along these lines. Here the children are encouraged to become highly dependent on their house-mothers and are permitted to regress to such infantile behaviour as taking their food from a baby's feeding-bottle. This, and similar experiments in the USA, are conceived on sensible lines, though there is debate regarding the optimal degree of control which should be exercised over the children. It will be many years before the success of these methods can be judged.

The evidence available suggests that nothing but prolonged residence with an adult, with insight into the problem, skill in handling it, and un-limited time to devote to her charge, is likely to be of much avail. This is not only very expensive but could never be made available to more than a tiny fraction of cases. Far more practicable, and in the long run far cheaper, is to arrange methods of care for infants and toddlers which will prevent these conditions developing.

CHAPTER 5

THEORETICAL PROBLEMS

The theoretical problems regarding personality development and its dependence on a continuous relationship with a nurturant figure during the critical period of ego and super-ego development in the early years are of the greatest interest. It would not be appropriate in this report to do more than touch on them, however, since they are very complex and by no means clearly understood. On the other hand, progress in understanding the practical issues involved is to a high degree dependent on progress in theoretical insight.

The development of the personality is a process whereby we become less and less at the mercy of our immediate environment and of its impact upon us, and more and more able to pursue our own goals, often over long periods of time, and to select and create our own environment. Such a process implies, among other things, a capacity to abstract common properties, to think in symbolic terms, and to plan ahead—all attributes of what Goldstein & Scheerer [69] have termed the abstract attitude. Only when this abstract attitude is developed has the individual the capacity to control his wish of the moment in the interests of his own more fundamental long-term needs. One expects the child of three, or even five, to run into the road to seek his ball—at those ages he is still largely at the mercy of the immediate situation. As he grows older, however, he is expected to take more things into account and to think ahead. By 10 or 11 he is capable of pursuing goals some months distant in time. At 16 or 18 the more developed boy or girl is able to perform prodigious feats of abstraction in time and space. Using psycho-analytic terms, this is the process whereby the individual frees himself from slavery to his instincts and the reign of the pleasure principle, and develops mental processes more adapted to the demands of reality.

The psychic machinery which we develop within ourselves to harmonize our different and often conflicting needs and to seek their satisfaction in a world realistically apprehended is our ego. Its functions are many and include appraisal of our long- and short-term needs, their arrangement in an order of priority, the inhibition of some and the acceptance of others, so that action may be purposeful and integrated instead of haphazard and self-frustrating. Because one of our foremost long-term needs is to remain on friendly and co-operative terms with others, we must keep their requirements firmly in the front of our minds ; and so important is this for us that we differentiate, within our ego, machinery specially designed for the purpose—our conscience or super-ego. It is evident that both ego and super-ego are absolutely dependent for their functioning on our ability to maintain the abstract attitude and it is not surprising that during infancy and early childhood these functions are either not operating at all or are doing so most imperfectly. During this phase of life, the child is therefore dependent on his mother performing them for him. She orients him in space and time, provides his environment, permits the satisfaction of some impulses, restricts others. She is his ego and his super-ego. Gradually he learns these arts himself and, as he does so, the skilled parent transfers the roles to him. This is a slow, subtle, and continuous process, beginning when he first learns to walk and feed himself and not ending completely until maturity is reached.

Ego and super-ego development are thus inextricably bound up with the child's primary human relationships ; only when these are continuous and satisfactory can his ego and super-ego develop. In dealing here with the embryology of the human mind one is struck by a similarity with the embryological development of the human body, during the course of which undifferentiated tissues respond to the influence of chemical organizers. If growth is to proceed smoothly, the tissues must be exposed to the influence of the appropriate organizer at certain critical periods. In the same way, if mental development is to proceed smoothly, it would appear to be necessary for the undifferentiated psyche to be exposed during certain critical periods to the influence of the psychic organizer—the mother. For this reason, in considering the disorders to which ego and super-ego are liable, it is imperative to have regard to the phases of development of the child's capacity for human relationships. These are many and, naturally, merge into one another. In broad outline the following are the most important :

(a) the phase during which the infant is in course of establishing a relation with a clearly identified person—his mother ; this is normally achieved by five or six months of age.

(b) The phase during which he needs her as an ever-present companion ; this usually continues until about his third birthday.

(c) The phase during which he is becoming able to maintain a relationship with her in absentia. During the fourth and fifth years such a relationship can only be maintained in favourable circumstances and for a few days or weeks at a time ; after seven or eight the relationship can be maintained, though not without strain, for periods of a year or more.

The process whereby he simultaneously develops his own ego and super-ego and the capacity to maintain relationships in absentia is variously described as a process of identification, internalization, or introjection, since the functions of ego and super-ego are incorporated within the self in the pattern set by the parents.

The ages by which these phases are completed no doubt vary greatly from child to child in the same way that physical maturation varies. For instance, the capacity to walk matures at any time between 9 and 24 months, and it may well be that psychic maturation is equally variable. If this is so, it will be wise to be concerned in research with developmental rather than chronological age, since it seems fairly certain that the kind and degree of psychological disorder following deprivation is dependent on the phase of development the child is in at the time. In postulating this, well-established embryological principles are again followed. As Corner [45] states :

" abnormalities are produced by attacking, at just the right time, a region in which profound growth activity is under way . . . Possible abnormalities will tend to fall into classes and types corresponding to the most critical stages and regions in development. Injuries inflicted early will in general produce widespread disturbance of growth . . . late injuries will tend on the other hand to produce local defects ".

Furthermore, he notes that

" a given undifferentiated tissue can respond to an organizer only during a limited period. It must have reached a certain stage of differentiation before it can respond ; and later its character becomes fixed, so that it can yield only a more limited type of response ".

The period during which the child's undifferentiated psyche can respond to the influence of the maternal ' organizer ' is similarly limited. Thus the evidence is fairly clear that if the first phase of development—that of establishing a relation with a clearly differentiated person—is not satisfactorily completed during the first 12 months or so, there is the greatest difficulty in making it good : the character of the psychic tissues has become fixed. (The limit for many children may well be a good deal earlier). Similarly, there appears to be a limit by which the second and third phases must be completed if further development is to proceed.

Now it is these vital growth processes which are impaired by the experience of deprivation. Clinically, it is observed that the egos and super-egos of severely deprived children are not developed—their behaviour is impulsive and uncontrolled, and they are unable to pursue long-term goals because they are the victims of the momentary whim. For them, all wishes are born equal and equally to be acted upon. Their capacity for inhibition is absent or impaired, and without this a limited, precise, and consequently efficient mode of response cannot develop. They are ineffective personalities, unable to learn from experience and consequently their own worst enemies.

The theoretical problem is to understand how deprivation produces this result. The two main approaches to its solution are Goldfarb's discoveries [62] regarding the impairment of abstract thinking in these patients, and the clinical findings regarding their inability to identify or introject. Each approach carries us some distance, but the day has yet to come when they lead to a unified body of theory.

Goldfarb's findings in regard to the serious and specific impairment of the capacity for abstract thinking, which was present in every one of his cases, might be held to explain the failure of ego and super-ego development, since, as already remarked, this capacity is of the essence of their functioning. But even if this is so there remains the puzzle as to why deprivation should impair the capacity for abstract thinking. One possibility is that this capacity not only underlies ego functioning, but can develop only if ego functioning itself develops favourably. This will need investigation.

The failure of ego development in deprived children is perhaps more easily understood when it is considered that it is the mother who in the child's earliest years fulfils the function of his ego and super-ego. The institution children studied by Goldfarb and by Bender had never had this experience, and so had never had the opportunity of completing the first phase of development—that of establishing a relationship with a clearly identified mother-figure. All they had had was a succession of ad hoc agents each helping them in some limited way, but none providing continuity in time, which is of the essence of ego functioning. It may well be that these grossly deprived infants, never having been the continuous objects of care of a single human being, had never had the opportunity to learn the processes of abstraction and of the organization of behaviour in time and space. Certainly their grave psychical deformities are clear examples of the principle that injuries inflicted early produce widespread disturbance of growth.

In the institutional setting, moreover, there is less opportunity for the child who has learnt the processes of abstraction and mental organization to exercise them. In the family, the young child is, within limits, encouraged to express himself both socially and in play. A child of 18 months or 2 years has already become a character in the family. It is known that he enjoys certain things and dislikes others, and the family has learnt to respect his wishes. Furthermore, he is getting to know how to get his parents or his brothers and sisters to do what he wants. In this way he is learning to change his social environment to a shape more congenial to him. The same occurs in his play, where in a symbolic way he is creating and recreating new worlds for himself. Here are the exercise grounds for ego and super-ego. In any institutional setting much of this is lost ; in the less good it may all be lost. The child is not encouraged to individual activity because it is a nuisance ; it is easier if he stays put and does what he is told. Even if he strives to change his environment he fails. Toys are lacking : often the children sit inert or rock themselves for hours together. Above all, the brief intimate games which mother and baby invent to amuse themselves as an accompaniment to getting up and washing, dressing, feeding, bathing, and returning to sleep—they are all missing. In these conditions, the child has no opportunity of learning and practising functions which are as basic to living as walking and talking.

The case of the child who has a good relation with his mother for a year or two and then suffers deprivation may be rather different. He has passed through the first phase of social development, that of establishing a relationship, and the trauma affects the second phase in which, though ego and super-ego development is proceeding apace, the child's awareness of his relative lack of skill in these matters is reflected in his limpet-like attachment to his mother, to whom he constantly looks for help. Only if she is with him or near at hand can he manage his environment and manage himself. If he is suddenly removed from her, to hospital or institution, he is faced with tasks which he feels to be impossible. In a traumatic situation of this kind it is usual for such skill as has already been learnt to be lost. There is usually a regression to primitive functioning and increased difficulty in learning afresh. This well-known principle of the theory of learning may account for the regression to and fixation of those children at primitive modes of thinking and behaviour, and their seeming inability to progress to more mature methods.

A further principle of the theory of learning is that an individual cannot learn a skill unless he has a friendly feeling towards his teacher, and is ready to identify himself with her and to incorporate her (or some part of her) into himself. Now this positive attitude towards his mother is either lacking in the deprived child or, if present, is mixed with keen resentment. How early in a child's life deprivation causes a specifically hostile attitude is debatable, but it is certainly evident for all to see in the second year. No observation is more common than that of the child separated for a few weeks or months during the second, third, and fourth years failing to recognize his mother on reunion. It seems probable that this is sometimes a true failure to recognize, based on a regression in the capacity to abstract and identify. At others, it is certain that it is a refusal to recognize, since the children, instead of treating their parents as though they were strangers, are deliberate in their avoidance of them. The parents have become hated people. This hostility is variously expressed. It may take the form of tempers and violence ; in older children it may be expressed verbally. All who have treated such children are familiar with the violence of their fantasies against the parents whom they feel have deserted them. Such an attitude is not only incompatible with their desire for love and security, and results in acute conflict, anxiety, and depression, but is clearly inimical to their future social learning. So far from idolizing their parents and wishing to become like them, one side of them hates them and wishes to avoid having anything to do with them. This is the dynamic of aggressively delinquent behaviour and may also be the dynamic of suicide, which is the result of the same conflict fought out between different systems within the self.

In other cases the child has suffered so much pain through making relationships and having them interrupted that he is reluctant ever again to give his heart to anyone for fear of its being broken. And not only his own heart : he is afraid too, to break the heart of new persons whom he might love because he might also vent his anger on them. Older children are sometimes aware of this and will remark to a therapist : " We had better not become too familiar, for I am afraid I shall get hostile with you then " (quoted by Tibout [141]). It is feelings such as these which underlie the withdrawal response. To withdraw from human contact is to avoid further frustration and to avoid the intense depression which human beings experience as a result of hating the person whom they most dearly love and need. Withdrawal is thus felt to be the better of two bad alternatives. Unfortunately, it proves to be a blind alley for no further development is then possible ; progress in human relations necessitates the individual taking the other road, in which he learns to tolerate his ambivalent feelings and to bear the anxiety and depression which go with them. But experience shows that once a person has taken refuge in the relative painlessness of withdrawal he is reluctant to change course and to risk the turmoil of feeling and misery which attempting relationships brings with it. As a result his capacity to make affectionate relationships and to identify with loved people becomes inhibited and any treatment offered is resisted. Thenceforward he becomes a lone wolf, pursuing his ends irrespective of others. But his desire for love, repressed though it is, persists, resulting in behaviour such as promiscuity and the stealing of other people's possessions. Feelings of revenge also smoulder on, leading to other antisocial acts, sometimes of a very violent character.

Deprivation after the age of three or four, namely in the third phase, does not have the same destructive effect on ego and super-ego development and on the ability for abstract thinking. It still results, however, in excessive desires for affection and excessive impulses for revenge, which cause acute internal conflict and unhappiness and very unfavourable social attitudes.

In both the second and third phases the child's restricted sense of time and his tendency to misapprehend a situation add greatly to his difficulties. It is exceedingly difficult for grown-ups to remember that the young child's grasp of time is meagre. The child of three can recall the events of a few days ago and anticipate those of a day or two hence. Notions such as last week or last month, next week or next month are incomprehensible. Even for a child of five or six, weeks are immensely long and months almost timeless. This very restricted time-span has to be understood if the despair which the young child feels at being left alone in a strange place is to be fully realized. Though to his mother it may seem not only a finite but relatively brief time, to him it is eternity. It is this inability to imagine a time of deliverance which, together with the sense of his helplessness, accounts for the overwhelming nature of his anxiety and despair. Perhaps the nearest to it the grown-up can conceive is to imagine being committed to prison on an indeterminate sentence.

This analogy is apt, since the notion of punishment is itself not far from many a child's mind as the explanation of events. All clinicians have come across children who have seriously believed that their being sent away from home was to punish them for being naughty, a misconstruction which is often made even more terrifying and distressing by being unexpressed. At other times children imagine that it has been their fault that the home has been broken up. Commonly there is bewilderment and perplexity regarding the course of events, which leads the child to be unable to accept and respond to his new environment and the new people caring for him. Naturally a child who has suffered gross privation in early infancy, or who for other reasons cannot make relationships, will not be affected in these ways, but will greet each change with the genial indifference apparent in Levy's case already quoted. But for the child who has had the opportunity to make relationships it is not so easy to change loyalties. Indeed, very many of the problems which arise as a result of moving an older child to a foster-home are caused by the failure to recognize the deep attachment which a child has for his parents, even if they are exceedingly bad and have given him little affection. Unless these perplexities are cleared up and these loyalties respected, the child will remain anchored in an unsatisfactory past, endlessly trying to find his mother and refusing to adapt to the new situation and make the best of it. This results in a dissatisfied restless character unable to make either himself or anyone else happy.

By and large, then, the theoretical framework of developmental phases of ego functioning and of capacity to make object relationships, and of the periods within the life cycle by which they must be completed, seems to fit the clinical evidence. No doubt as understanding increases the three main phases described here will be subdivided into many subphases, and one will learn to discern the particular psychic forces which are brought into play by deprivation in each of them.

In this brief sketch no attempt has been made to go into detail nor to compare and discuss the views of the many psycho-analysts and psychologists who have contributed to our understanding. Those familiar with the literature will know where the writer's debts lie.

CHAPTER 6

RESEARCH INTO EFFECTS OF DEPRIVATION

It is now demonstrated that maternal care in infancy and early child-hood is essential for mental health. This is a discovery comparable in magnitude to that of the role of vitamins in physical health, and of far-reaching significance for programmes of preventive mental hygiene. On this new understanding social measures of great consequence for the future will be based. These measures will only be wisely planned, however, if knowledge of what is essential and what is not is progressively increased.

Not only is further research in the field necessary to guide immediate preventive measures, but it promises also to cast light on some of the fundamental problems of personality development, on the understanding of which all the social sciences depend. Personality growth is the result of an interaction between the growing organism and other human beings. In some way the organism assimilates features of its social environment, and in so doing grows increasingly like its culture medium, though it is ever an unique synthesis of the social material of which it is made. How this process of psychic assimilation proceeds is not understood. Deprivation in infancy and early childhood is an experience which deranges it to a severe degree, and in the history of medicine it has often been the study of gross dysfunction which has most clearly illuminated the nature of the function itself. It may well be that in studying these grave derangements of the assimilatory process a clearer light will be thrown on this central process of personality growth.

Whether research in this field is undertaken with a view to promoting better preventive measures or greater fundamental understanding, hence-forward it should be regarded as unnecessary to spend time demonstrating the validity of the general proposition respecting the adverse effects of deprivation. Instead, the research worker should be encouraged to move on, both to the study of basic processes and to the identification and unra-velling of the effects of the many variables operating. Though aware of some of them—age and emotional development of the child, length of deprivation, degree of deprivation, relations with mother-figure before and after deprivation—there are, no doubt, some of which we are still ignorant. Matters of immediate practical significance on which information is needed are the lengths of the safety margin (a) during which deprivation can, if absolutely necessary, be permitted, and (b) within which there is time to make good damage already done. On the theoretical side, as the previous chapter has shown, investigators are still far from clear on the principles of psychic metabolism, without which their mode of action cannot be understood. Working hypotheses, however, can be erected and these should be elaborated in some detail so that clear formulations are made which can be tested. There is no place for systematic research unguided by explicit hypotheses.

In addition to the problems of theoretical clarification, there are immense problems of execution. In the first place, it is not possible cold-bloodedly to arrange for children to be deprived of mothering at various ages and for various periods. To a high degree the investigator is dependent on experiments of opportunity, in which groups of children who for one reason or another are being or have been subject to this experience are discovered and studied. Ideally, to isolate the effects of deprivation, all other factors known to be emotionally disturbing would be absent from the cases. Thus the ideal sample would consist of healthy children of good parentage, who, so long as they were with their mothers, would have enjoyed good relationships with them. The reason for separation, moreover, would not be traumatic in itself, while the conditions obtaining during separation would be carefully regulated. In practice few of these ideal research conditions hold. Deprived children are often sick and many are born of unstable or defective parents. Family relationships while they last leave much to be desired and the home is commonly broken because of destitution, neglect, or death. Many of the children are illegitimate and unwanted. Psychological conditions in institutions or foster-homes cannot easily be arranged to suit the research worker.

A further major difficulty is that of access. Detailed studies of infants in their homes and of their relations to their mothers require a degree of intimate contact not easily attained by the professional observer. Even when these infants are in institutions, the susceptibilities of the workers who are caring for them may impede objective study. Finally, parents who are anxious and guilty about their children's later behaviour may resent further inquiry.

There are no simple ways round these difficulties. Samples can be more carefully selected than has sometimes been the case in the past, however. Now that so much is understood regarding the theory of small samples, the large heterogeneous sample with many gaps in its data must be regarded as a thing of the past. No amount of statistical analysis will remedy data which are inadequate and inaccurate. The small, homogeneous, and carefully matched samples of the kind studied by Goldfarb are far more likely to give unequivocal answers. Each sample can then be selected from all the deprived children available to conform to some extent to certain defined criteria. It will be possible, for instance, to avoid children of bad heredity or those who have had unhappy experiences in their homes. The age at which a child first experiences deprivation can be held constant, though it may be necessary to wait some time before finding sufficient cases to fulfil these criteria and to cover all age-groups. To regulate the child's experiences while in an institution is more difficult, though, in the main, it will be possible to select places where insightful attempts are being made to provide substitute care and others where such attempts are not being made. Other variables difficult to control are the length of time the child is in an institution and what happens to him afterwards. Suffice it to say that only planned investigations of large numbers of very carefully selected cases are likely to unravel the influences of all these variables.

The problem of access, to permit the observation of relevant data, is present in all psychological studies of human beings which are not content with superficial description and, instead, seek to understand motivation, since people habitually hide many of their feelings especially those about which they are anxious and guilty. The only key yet found to unlock these secrets is the therapeutic approach, in which the research worker holds himself in readiness to help his subjects should they wish it. Naturally many will not respond, but others, sensing that the research worker is ready to aid them as well as to study them, will give him opportunities for both.

Fortunately, the problems both of sampling and of access are absent if we use animals as our experimental subjects, as Liddell is doing. At present he is studying goats, but it might be that dogs would be more rewarding subjects, since much of a practical kind is already known about their social development. For instance, it is a commonplace that a sporting dog must be trained by one master who must feed him himself, and that there are difficulties of transfer to a new master. Starting with the knowledge already available, it should be relatively easy to construct a series of experiments and perhaps gain insights which could then be tested with human beings.

A research team working on these problems, whether with animals or humans and preferably with both, needs to be equipped with many different techniques of observation, since each technique, whatever its value, has strict limitations. Only by ensuring that data derived from one source are complemented by data derived from others is all the necessary information likely to be obtained. It is especially important to combine the experimental, the psychometric, and the clinical approaches, since each can give indispensable data not provided by the others. In the past there has been a deplorable tendency for the experimentalist to despise the clinician's lack of precision and the clinician to reciprocate with contempt for the experimentalist's lack of insight into human nature. Each has stoutly maintained that his own method was the one true way to knowledge. These claims are absurd : each method is indispensable. It is the clinician who usually has the earliest insights, defines the problem, and formulates the first hypotheses. By the detailed minute study of the feelings and motivations of his patients, and the complicated intellectual and emotional repercussions to which they give rise, the clinical worker provides information regarding the relations of psychic and environmental forces which can be obtained in no other way. This is the first sketch-map, which, though erroneous in many particulars, gives an invaluable overall picture of the new territory. (In elucidating the adverse effects of maternal deprivation it is no accident that psycho-analysts and clinical workers closely associated with them played a leading part.) The clinician is rarely in a position, however, or scientifically qualified, to test the hypotheses he has advanced : the next step must be done in more-controlled conditions by those with other skills.   The planned experimental and psychometric study of statistically significant samples of subjects gives information regarding the validity of hypotheses which no amount of clinical work can give.   Similarly, systematic work will in its turn lead to hypotheses, some of which can be profitably studied in a clinical setting before plans to verify them are elaborated.   This combination of clinical and experimental techniques, in which work of each kind is designed to complement and promote work of the other, is the way to future progress. But it means that each type of worker must learn to understand the merits of the others' skills and the limitations of his own.   Surveys and experimental work must be planned and executed using all the insight the clinician can supply.   Equally, the clinician must select for study just those cases which the statistically trained worker indicates are likely to give most understanding of the problems selected for study, and must also concern himself with the recording and reliability of data, which has not been his strongest point in the past.   Only by working together in a common team will the experimental psychologist, the statistician, the psycho-analyst, the psychometrist, and those with other trainings learn to respect each other and to mobilize to the greatest advantage all the skills available.

In addition to utilizing all the psychological techniques, there is good reason to include techniques of physiological measurement.   The probable value of the Wetzel Grid has already been noted.   Electro-encephalographic studies may also be of great interest.   For instance, it is known that there is a similarity in the (abnormal) electro-encephalograms of aggressive psychopathic adolescents and those of normal young children between the ages of three and five.   Though it is commonly assumed that these abnormal cerebral rhythms are due to a physical factor, as for instance genetic defect or birth injury, there are no data to support such an assumption and they may prove to be psychogenic in origin and in the nature of a fixation at an earlier level of functioning.   If further inquiries proved this to be the case, a valuable link would have been made between psychopathology and neurophysiology.

Clearly then here, in the embryology of personality, is a field rich and ripe for research and one to be exploited to the full before increasingly effective preventive measures have robbed the research worker of his clinical material. The growth of an individual proceeds by differentiation "from large diffuse unfocused responses to goal determined, limited, precise and consequently efficient modes of response" (Goldfarb [62]). In his search for clearer understanding and more precisely adapted action, the scientist proceeds similarly, moving from the perception of certain general and gross relationships to a finer and finer appreciation of the nature of the forces at work and of their influence on each other. In the field of mental health and its relation to parental care investigators have so far done no more than perceive the gross relationships. It is for workers in the coming half-century to refine perceptions, to elucidate complexities, and to give the power to prevent mental illness.

Part II

PREVENTION OF MATERNAL DEPRIVATION

CHAPTER 7

THE PURPOSE OF THE FAMILY

The demonstration that maternal deprivation in the early years has an adverse effect on personality growth is a challenge to action. How can this deprivation be prevented so that children may grow up mentally healthy ?

It was said at the beginning of the first chapter that what is believed to be essential for mental health is that the infant and young child should experience a warm, intimate, and continuous relationship with his mother (or mother-substitute), in which both find satisfaction and enjoyment. The child needs to feel he is an object of pleasure and pride to his mother ; the mother needs to feel an expansion of her own personality in the personality of her child : each needs to feel closely identified with the other. The mothering of a child is not something which can be arranged by roster; it is a live human relationship which alters the characters of both partners. The provision of a proper diet calls for more than calories and vitamins : we need to enjoy our food if it is to do us good. In the same way the provision of mothering cannot be considered in terms of hours per day but only in terms of the enjoyment of each other's company which mother and child obtain.

Such enjoyment and close identification of feeling is only possible for either party if the relationship is continuous. Much emphasis has already been laid on the necessity of continuity for the growth of a child's personality. It should be remembered, too, that continuity is necessary for the growth of a mother. Just as the baby needs to feel that he belongs to his mother, the mother needs to feel that she belongs to her child and it is only when she has the satisfaction of this feeling that it is easy for her to devote herself to him. The provision of constant attention day and night, seven days a week and 365 in the year, is possible only for a woman who derives profound satisfaction from seeing her child grow from babyhood, through the many phases of childhood, to become an independent man or woman, and knows that it is her care which has made this possible.

It is for these reasons that the mother-love which a young child needs is so easily provided within the family, and is so very very difficult to provide outside it. The services which mothers and fathers habitually render their children are so taken for granted that their magnitude is forgotten. In no other relationship do human beings place themselves so unreservedly and so continuously at the disposal of others. This holds true even of bad parents—a fact far too easily forgotten by their critics, especially critics who have never had the care of children of their own. It must never be forgotten that even the bad parent who neglects her child is none the less providing much for him. Except in the worst cases, she is giving him food and shelter, comforting him in distress, teaching him simple skills, and above all is providing him with that continuity of human care on which his sense of security rests. He may be ill-fed and ill-sheltered, he may be very dirty and suffering from disease, he may be ill-treated, but, unless his parents have wholly rejected him, he is secure in the knowledge that there is *someone* to whom he is of value and who will strive, even though inadequately, to provide for him until such time as he can fend for himself.

It is against this background that the reason why children thrive better in bad homes than in good institutions and why children with bad parents are, apparently unreasonably, so attached to them can be understood. Those responsible for institutions have sometimes been resistant to acknowledging that children are often better off in even quite bad homes, which is the conclusion of most experienced social workers with mental health training and is borne out by the evidence of Simonsen and of Theis, already quoted. Simonsen,[130] it will be remembered, compared a group of children aged between one and four years who had spent their lives in institutions with a comparable group who lived in their, often very unsatisfactory, homes and spent the day in day nurseries because their mothers were working. The difference in mean developmental quotient was 9 points in favour of the children living at home and attending day-nursery (see page 19). In her follow-up study Theis[139] compared the social adjustment in adult life of children who had spent five years or more of their childhood in institutions with others who had spent the same years at home—in 80% of cases in bad homes. The results, given in table VIII (see page 40) clearly favour the bad homes, those growing up to be socially incapable being only about half (18%) of those from institutions (34.5%).

That one-third of all those who had spent five years or more of their lives in institutions turned out to be ' socially incapable ' in adult life is alarming, and no less alarming in the light of the reflection that one of the principal social functions of an adult is that of parenthood. For one may be reasonably sure that all the 34% of Theis' institution children who grew up to be ' socially incapable ' adults were incapable as parents, and one may suspect that some at least of those who were not grossly incapable socially still left much to be desired as parents. Yet, incapable as parents though they may have been, it is unlikely that they were childless. On the contrary, many must have had children and many of these children must have been neglected and deprived. Thus it is seen how children who suffer deprivation grow up to become parents deficient in the capacity to care for their children, and how adults deficient in this capacity are commonly those who suffered deprivation in childhood. This vicious circle is the most serious aspect of the problem and one to which this report will constantly revert.

Naturally the evidence from the work of Theis and of Simonsen—that bad homes are often better than good institutions—is far from definitive and in any case all depends on how bad is the home and how good the institution. Nevertheless, they serve as a reminder that there may be something worse than a bad home—and that is no home. As Spence [131] has pointed out in his inspiring lecture, carrying a title which has been borrowed to name this chapter, one of the principal purposes of the family is the preservation of the art of parenthood. Unless this art is preserved, a function as necessary to the preservation of society as the production of food will fall into decay. Yet the merits of particular methods of child upbringing are rarely judged by the performance as parents of the children they rear ; in particular this criterion seems never to have been applied to measure the success or failure of methods at present used for the care of children deprived of a normal home life.

The attachment of children to parents who by all ordinary standards are very bad is a never-ceasing source of wonder to those who seek to help them. Even when they are with kindly foster-parents these children feel their roots to be in the homes where, perhaps, they have been neglected and ill-treated, and keenly resent criticisms directed against their parents. Efforts made to ' save ' the child from his bad surroundings and to give him new standards are commonly of no avail since it is his own parents who, for good or ill, he values and with whom he is identified. (This is a fact of critical importance when considering how best to help children who are living in intolerable home conditions.) These sentiments are not surprising when it is remembered that, despite much neglect, one or other parent has almost always and in countless ways been kind to him from the day of his birth onwards, and, however much the outsider sees to criticize, the child sees much to be grateful for. At least his parents have cared for him after a fashion all his life, and not until someone else has shown herself equally or more dependable has he reason to trust her. Unfortunately, he is usually right in his mistrust. Once a child is out of his own home he is lucky if he finds someone who will care for him till he is grown up. Even for good foster-home agencies the rate of replacement is deplorably high ; even in good institutions the turnover of staff is a constant problem. However devoted foster-parents or house-mothers may be, they have not the same sense of absolute obligation to the child which all but the worst parents possess. When other interests and duties call the foster-child takes second place. The child is therefore right to distrust them—from his point of view there is no one like his own parents.

This conclusion was reached by the British Ministry of Health [76] in its survey of the lessons of evacuating children from the dangers of bombing during the second World War :

" One point which all experience in the evacuation scheme has emphasized is the importance of the family in a child's development and the impossibility of providing children with any completely adequate substitute for the care of their own parents. This has led to an increased awareness in some quarters of the importance of improving home conditions in order to keep families together instead of removing children from unsatisfactory homes."

A warning that the decision to remove a child from his own home is one of great gravity was given 20 years ago by a distinguished quartet of American psychiatrists and social workers : [77]

" The decision which for any cause separates a child from his family is very serious ; it sets in motion events which to a greater or lesser degree affect the whole of his future life. Whether the removal is due to sickness, neglect, desertion, inefficiency, or death of parents, or to the child's conduct inside or outside the home, the transfer to the control of strangers should not be made without much forethought . . . Too often children are taken from their families with very little, if any, study of the causes that lie behind the situation. Many agencies mistakenly approach the problem with predetermined ideas of the conditions which would warrant removal rather than with the purpose of ascertaining whether the home of the parents can be made suitable for the child. "

It is salutary to note that, though this was written 20 years ago, its message is as timely today as it was then. It is still common in Western communities to see in the removal of the child from home the solution to many a family problem without there being any appreciation of the gravity of the step and, often, without there being any clear plan for the future. It is too often forgotten that in removing a child of five from home direct responsibility is taken for his future health and happiness for a decade to come, and that in removing an infant the crippling of his character is at risk.

From all this the trite conclusion is reached that family life is of pre-eminent importance and that ' there's no place like home '. But, trite though it may be, its truth is often flouted and, judging by the meagre and confused literature on the subject, little attention has been given to the conditions making for family prosperity and family decay. Since the basic method of preventing a child suffering maternal deprivation must be to ensure that he receives nurture within his own family, it is necessary to consider these matters in some detail. This is a departure from the tradition set by reports on deprived children, which have given scant attention to methods by which home conditions may be improved so that families may remain together and which have, instead, hurried on to consider how best to arrange for their care elsewhere. On this topic a great literature of reports and textbooks has grown up, all assuming that homeless children are an inevitable feature of social life and most of them content to discuss their care without reference to the reasons for which they come into care. It must, of course, be recognized that on occasion children have to be cared for outside their own homes, but let such arrangements be regarded as a last resort to be undertaken only when it is absolutely impossible for the home to be made fit for the child.

In pausing to inquire the reasons for family care failing, or appearing to fail, to provide for the child, the investigator will find himself in a largely unexplored field which can be properly surveyed only by a team possessing more than psychiatric skills. Nevertheless, it will be found that psychiatric knowledge is indispensable if the problems discovered are to be understood and he will be tempted to the conclusion that it has been largely because psychiatric understanding has not been brought to bear that so little progress has hitherto been made.

Three interrelated circumstances in which a child suffers maternal deprivation may be distinguished :

(a) the partial deprivation of living with a mother or permanent mother-substitute, including a relative, whose attitude towards him is unfavourable;

(b) the complete deprivation of losing his mother (or permanent mother-substitute) by death, illness, or desertion and having no familiar relatives to care for him ;

(c) the complete deprivation of being removed from his mother (or permanent mother-substitute) to strangers by medical or social agencies.

Naturally cases coming under (a) above are very numerous and of all degrees of severity from the child whose mother leaves him to scream for many hours because the baby-books tell her to do so to infants whose mothers wholly reject them. The partial forms of maternal deprivation, due sometimes to ignorance but more often to unconscious hostility on the part of the mother deriving from experiences in her own childhood, could well form the subject of another report. Many child-guidance workers believe they comprise a large fraction of all the cases they are called upon to treat, and that the process of helping the mother to appreciate her true feelings for the child and their origins in her own childhood is an essential part of their treatment—in other words that parent treatment is an essential part of child guidance. However, this report has for its purpose the consideration of the grosser forms of deprivation and it is to the prevention of these that attention will be given. The great majority of them are the result of family failure, and for this reason the focus will be on cases where the child never had a family, where his family has broken down, or where social agencies have removed him from his home because it has been judged to have failed. However, in addition to these, there is a sufficient number of cases where, owing to maladjustment or physical illness, children are removed from home under medical or legal auspices, and are thus deprived of maternal care, for it to be necessary to give them some separate consideration, even though it is not infrequent for these conditions themselves to be the result of family failure.

CHAPTER 8

CAUSES OF FAMILY FAILURE IN WESTERN COMMUNITIES, WITH SPECIAL REFERENCE TO PSYCHIATRIC FACTORS

Definitions which attempt to describe ‘ normal home life ’ in terms of family structure are seen to be inadequate. Not only is it clearly understood both by the Curtis [72] and the League of Nations Reports [90] that a child can have a normal home life when living with relatives other than his parents, but it is obvious that a child can be living with his own parents and yet not be getting a normal home life. It is evident that the definition must be in *functional* terms.

It is because a young child is not an organism capable of independent life that he requires a special social institution to aid him during his period of immaturity. This social institution must aid him in two main ways : first, by helping in the satisfaction of immediate biological needs such as nutrition, warmth and shelter, and protection from danger ; secondly, by providing a milieu in which he may develop his physical, mental, and social capacities to the full so that, when grown up, he may be able to deal with his physical and social environment effectively. This demands an atmosphere of affection and security.

Traditions as to who normally performs these indispensable functions of child care vary from community to community. In most, the child's natural mother and father play leading parts, though even this is not always the case. Traditions vary especially in regard to the extent to which there are accepted substitutes for mother and father readily available. In many of the less-developed communities, people live in large family groups comprising three or four generations. Near and known relatives—grandmothers, aunts, older sisters—are thus always at hand to take the maternal role in an emergency. Economic support, moreover, is forthcoming if the bread-winner is incapacitated. The greater family group living together in one locality provides a social insurance system of great value. Even in Western communities, there are many rural pockets in which close-knit and much inter-married village groups provide similar social services for their members. It is probably only in communities in which the greater family group has ceased to exist that the problem of deprived children is found on a serious scale. This condition characterizes many communities of Western industrialized culture, in which it is usual for young men and women to migrate far from their birthplaces and, not infrequently, to move many times in the course of their married lives. As a result of such migrations very many families have such loose ties with their local societies that for whole communities it has ceased to be a tradition to help a neighbour in distress. As a result of this social fragmentation, of which Mumford [107] and others have written, a far heavier responsibility for child care is placed on the father and mother than is the case in more primitive, close-knit communities. Not only does such a fragmented community provide no substitutes should the mother or father be temporarily or permanently incapacitated but, by putting this great load on parents, it may disrupt a family which in better circumstances could hold together.

In Western communities today it is the tradition that ' normal home life ' is provided by the child's mother and father, which is conveniently described as the child's ' natural home group '. Despite social fragmentation, it still remains the tradition (though less strong than formerly) that, if this group fails for any reason, near relatives take responsibility for the child. In any analysis of the causes of children becoming deprived, therefore, it has to be considered not only why the natural home group has failed, but also why relatives have failed to act as substitutes.

Causes of the Natural Home Group Failing to Care for the Child

These are conveniently grouped under three heads according to the state of the natural home group :

(1) Natural home group never established :

   Illegitimacy

(2) Natural home group intact but not functioning effectively :

   Economic conditions leading to unemployment of breadwinner with consequent poverty

   Chronic illness or incapacity of parent

   Instability or psychopathy of parent

(3) Natural home group broken up and therefore not functioning:

   Social calamity—war, famine

   Death of a parent

   Illness requiring hospitalization of a parent

   Imprisonment of a parent

   Desertion by one or both parents

   Separation or divorce

   Employment of father elsewhere

   Full-time employment of mother.

Any family suffering from one or more of these conditions must be regarded as a potential source of deprived children. Whether or not these children actually become deprived will depend on (a) whether both or only one parent is affected, (b) whether, if only one parent is affected, help is given to the other, and (c) whether relatives or neighbours are able and willing to act as substitutes. The causes leading to deprivation in any particular case cannot be regarded as adequately presented unless information is available on all these points.

It is at present impossible to obtain even reasonably satisfactory figures giving the proportions of children deprived of a normal home life on account of these different conditions and of combinations of them. The obscurity is particularly notable in the second group where the natural home group is still in existence but for some reason not functioning effectively. Terms such as sloth, neglect, destitution, lack of parental control, cruelty are used, which do little more than describe the symptoms of the failure without in any way accounting for it. Notes of the factors responsible for such conditions, especially ill-health and mental instability, both of which are now known to be of great importance, are conspicuous by their absence. Similarly, under the third heading, death of a parent or desertion is frequently regarded as sufficient without even stating whether it is the father or the mother who has died or deserted, let alone the circumstances preventing the other caring for the child. It is very much to be hoped that as a result of the report of the Social Commission of the United Nations on this subject it may be possible to design more adequate categories of the causes of deprivation and of relatives failing to act as substitutes, and so to collect figures which are at once informative and comparable with others.

It is not possible in this report to attempt a thorough survey of whatever statistics exist. To obtain some idea of the proportions of the problem, however, certain figures which happened to be easily available, comprising four samples from the United Kingdom,[24, 29, 109, 110] two (one unpublished) from the USA,[100] and one from Sweden [140] are given in Appendix 4.[j] The main conclusions to be drawn from them, and from discussions with experienced social workers, appear to be as follows :

(a) The death of one or both parents is no longer of overriding importance, largely due to low death-rates for adults of child-bearing age and schemes of assistance for widows with children. Such cases probably account for less than 25% of all cases. In two of the largest samples, one British and the other American, the percentages were 10 and 6 respectively.

(b) Illegitimacy features prominently in all sets of figures, varying from about 10% to 40%. In homes for infants and children under 6 in Denmark in about 1945 the percentage was 80.[130]

(c) The natural home group being existent but not functioning effectively, resulting in ' neglect ', ' destitution ', ' lack of parental control ', or ' maladjustment of child ', is prominent in all but one set of figures and shows this condition to be the greatest single cause today. Poverty, neglect,

---

j See page 170

and lack of parental control account for 60% of cases in one large British sample while maladjustment of the child is responsible for 26% of cases in a New York sample.

(d) Where the natural home group is broken up, separation and divorce are common factors, varying from about 5% to 25% of all cases.

(e) Another important cause of the break-up of the natural home group is prolonged illness of a parent, necessitating hospitalization (or, in the case of mental defectives, institutionalization). Mental illness and defect predominate and probably account for some 5% to 10% of all cases.

(f) A situation has arisen in the United Kingdom in which it is now legally possible for parents who have been evicted for not paying their rent to leave the children in the care of a local authority and to find accommodation for themselves where children are not accepted. In one area this accounts for about 33% of the children in care.

Most of these immediate causes of children needing care have hitherto been accepted fatalistically as an inevitable part of social life, and until recent years no attempt was made to look beyond them into the underlying factors at work. Are illegitimacy, neglect, maladjustment, and desertion to be accepted as unavoidable social evils, or is there some prospect of understanding the forces promoting them and of combating them ? It is the thesis of this report that the present increased knowledge of human nature and of the part which family life plays in its development gives many and valuable clues to the understanding of the forces at work. The totality of these forces can be grouped broadly under the headings economic, social, and medical : the economic comprise the opportunities, or lack of opportunities, the family has for earning an adequate livelihood ; the social, the social system within which it lives and which provides greater or less support ; and the medical, the mental and physical health of the parents which determine what use is made of the opportunities offered. It is at once evident that the relative contributions of these three sets of forces will vary enormously from one community to another and, in the same community, from one period of time to another. Sometimes the economic forces will preponderate, sometimes the social or the medical, and at all times they will interact. No attempt is made here to discuss the economic forces at work. In what follows an attempt has been made to explore the nature and effects of the social and medical forces and to give special attention to psychiatric factors.

There is no group of children in danger of deprivation in whose production psychiatric factors play a larger part than illegitimates. For this reason, and because the care of illegitimates raises special problems, a separate chapter has been given to them. The present chapter will be concerned with the psychiatric factors conducing to the natural home group either breaking up or, although intact, failing to function effectively.

Considering that personality disturbances, especially in mothers, almost certainly play the principal part in a majority of the cases coming into care in Western communities today, it is remarkable that so little attention has hitherto been given to them. They are of particular importance in contributing to such diverse conditions as neglect, cruelty, the prolonged ill-health of a parent, lack of parental control, unhappy marriage, desertion, separation, and divorce. Each of these will be discussed in turn, note being taken of the contributions to their origin of psychiatric disabilities in the parents and the part played by deprivation and unhappiness in the childhoods of those parents.

Neglect

Cases in which parents are deemed to be neglecting their children are heterogeneous. Often the failure is in respect of physical care only and many experienced social workers have testified to the frequency with which children who have been ' neglected ' in the sense of their being dirty and ill-nourished are in excellent mental health and have clearly not suffered from the deprivation of love. Unfortunately, so preoccupied with physical health, and it might be added physical appearance, have workers sometimes been that the paradox has been witnessed of expensive social action being taken to convert a physically neglected but psychologically well-provided child into a physically well-provided but emotionally starved one.

At least two forms of neglect can therefore be recognized—physical neglect and emotional neglect—and, though they may often co-exist, it is of prime importance to distinguish them since they need very different therapeutic measures. Broadly speaking it will be found that, while physical neglect is most often due to economic factors, the ill-health of the mother, and ignorance, emotional neglect is the result of emotional instability and psychopathy in the parents. Mental defect may contribute to both.

The causes of parents who are living together neglecting their children was the subject of a report published in 1948 by a group of English women under the chairmanship of the late Eva Hubback.[110] While it is suggested that in England in the years 1946-1947 external and economic factors were not the principal cause, and that personal factors in the parents were of more substantial importance, it unfortunately failed to discuss these personal factors in much detail. Though the data on which its conclusions are based are far from satisfactory, there is no evidence of undue preoccupation with psychiatric factors—indeed the reverse is probably the case.

External and economic factors are discussed under four main heads, the principal conclusions being as follows :

Poverty : " Insufficient income was not generally considered to be directly responsible for neglect in the larger number of cases ", though " complete inability . . . to manage the household budget . . . clearly may be a cause, and there were many examples of foolish spending ".

Size of family : " Most witnesses were of the opinion that child-neglect in large families is no greater than in small ", but " there is abundant evidence . . . that pregnancies too close together " can undermine the mother's health.

Bad housing conditions : Though " there can be no doubt that bad housing can accentuate difficulties already existent ", it was none the less reported " that the homes where child-neglect was frequently found were not slum property nor poky hovels ".

Mother normally working : They found " no conclusive evidence that this was a cause of neglect " (pages 55-59).

In other Western communities it may well be that unemployment with inadequate insurance systems and consequent poverty are a major cause of a family going downhill, ultimately leading to neglect, but such conditions were apparently not common in England when this report was written. On the other hand, the report emphasizes the importance of physical and mental ill-health, both of which, it believes, have been greatly underestimated in the past.

" There is reason to believe that a wider study of women guilty of neglecting their children would confirm that not only do they not enjoy the kind of robust good health which would make their task possible, but that many would be in very poor health indeed . . . There is . . . a widespread failure to recognize psychological factors. People look for bad housing, poverty, and overcrowding as reasons for neglect. Too seldom do they take into account emotional conflict or abnormality " (page 60).

These are also the conclusions of the various medical officers of health who have investigated ' problem families ', namely families which exhibit a multiplicity of social problems, among which persistent child neglect is prominent, and which do not respond to ordinary measures of social aid. Blacker [21] has presented a useful review of the English literature and also refers to Querido's work in the Netherlands. The parents in problem families, especially the mothers, are found to be characterized by ineducability and instability of character. Though mental defect is not infrequent —both Wofinden [153] in an urban district of England and Savage [128] in a rural one found mental defect or near mental defect in about 25% of the mothers of problem families—it is agreed that this is not the major problem. Both Blacker and Mrs. Hubback's group point out that many borderline defectives make satisfactory parents if circumstances are reasonably favourable and familiar and they do not have too many children. " Distinguishable from the mental subnormality ", writes Blacker, " there is often present in either or both parents, but commonly in the mother, a temperamental instability which expresses itself in fecklessness, irresponsibility, improvidence and indiscipline in the home." In more theoretical terms it may be said that what is lacking is the capacity to adopt the abstract attitude. Describing the situation in the home, Querido [118] writes : " There are no papers, no books, no clock or calendar or other things of rule or order . . .

There is no attempt at planning or saving. When money is obtained, it is immediately expended, often on expensive delicacies." It is clearly this fundamental inability to function abstractly, to consider matters other than those of the moment, which explains much of the instability and psychopathy and which accounts for their lack of response to education and other measures designed to help them. Both Querido and Wofinden [154] state that, in their experience, bad housing has very little to do with the problem—it is the ineducable psychopathic character which is the heart of it.

Apart from these unchanging character disorders, which may lead to gross neglect, are the more transient conditions of anxiety and depression which, if present in a mother, may lead her to neglect her household duties, resulting in the home gradually deteriorating into a slum. Her loving feelings for the children may cease or may become infused with impatience and bitterness. Though such a condition is really an illness requiring medical attention, it frequently goes undiagnosed until the home has sunk below tolerable limits, in which circumstances it is more likely to be regarded as a social offence.

Discussions with social workers prominent in child care in the USA have again and again emphasized the importance of the emotional problems in the parents as being a major cause of children being in need of care and have emphasized, too, the extent to which deprivation and unhappiness in the parents' own childhoods have been the cause of their present problems. The psychopathic and unstable parent met as the cause of child neglect is clearly as often as not the grown-up affectionless psychopathic child, who has been discussed at length as being the typical product of maternal deprivation. Here again are the fickleness and irresponsibility, the inability to adopt an abstract attitude or to learn, the inaccessibility to help, the superficial relationships, the promiscuous sexual behaviour, with all of which the reader will have already become familiar. Admittedly, many such problem parents do not show all these features—in some the disability may be only partial—but of the basic identity there can be no doubt. This social succession—of the neglected psychopathic child growing up to become the neglectful psychopathic parent—has hitherto received little attention : on the contrary, the impression is given that those investigating problem families have been more concerned with possible heritable characteristics as accounting for the psychopathy of parents than with the events of their early childhoods. Because research workers have not so far given attention to this aspect of the matter, well-authenticated data are scarce. The main thesis is borne out, however, by the analysis [110] of 234 pairs of parents who had contributed 346 children to Dr. Barnardo's Homes in the years 1937-1939. It is true that in 60% of the mothers and 76% of the fathers no information regarding the parents' background was available, but this in itself is an important pointer, because, as the investigators state : " We have the impression that this type of parent has led an unsettled life, lacking permanent connexions, which makes a full case history impossible " (page 49). In the cases where some information is available the results are as set out in table XI.

TABLE XI. CHILDHOOD CIRCUMSTANCES OF PARENTS OF CHILDREN COMMITTED TO CARE (DR. BARNARDO'S HOMES)

Childhood circumstances	Mothers	Fathers
	%	%
Illegitimate	3	4
Institution	6	2
Abnormal childhood	49	25
Normal childhood	42	69
	100	100
Number of cases	97	53

" Abnormal childhood ", it is stated, " refers to parents who were reared in an atmosphere not conducive to healthy development, such as a broken home or dire poverty. Generally they would have come into our categories N[eglect], W[ilful] N[eglect], or C[ruelty], during childhood. The majority in this class are physically or mentally handicapped " (page 49). Thus 58% of the mothers and 31% of the fathers about whom there is information are known to have been deprived of a normal home life in their own childhood. Though these data are by no means wholly reliable there is no reason to suspect that they err on the side of exaggerating factors of psychiatric significance. It is to be hoped that this lead in the understanding of the origins of problem parents will be given due attention in future research.

Physical cruelty

Mercifully this is rare, accounting for no more than 3% to 5% of children in care. Though no psychiatric study of the personalities and childhood histories of parents guilty of this behaviour seems to have been undertaken, clinical experience of schoolchildren referred on account of their cruel behaviour to others shows them to be suffering from severe maladjustment, almost always resulting from gross deprivation or rejection. Cruelty to animals and other children is a characteristic, though not common, feature of the affectionless psychopath, and occasional outbursts of senseless cruelty are well known in schizophrenics and pre-schizophrenics. It is, therefore, probably safe to predict that when a study of parents guilty of physical cruelty to their children is made, personality disturbances

6

will prove the rule, either following a history of deprivation or rejection in childhood, or associated with a schizoid illness.

Prolonged ill-health of a parent

The contribution of chronic ill-health in a parent, especially the mother, to the causes of children becoming deprived has been much underrated in the past. Once again, moreover, attention must be called to psychiatric factors since, as a leading American authority, Hopkirk,[78] has stated : " mental disease of a parent is one of the most common of the factors leading to child dependency " (page 8), whether the mother is in a mental hospital or not. Because of its frequency and long duration, mental illness often plays an even larger part than physical illness in leading children to become in need of care ; for, not only does undiagnosed neurosis and psychopathy in the mother underlie much neglect of children in their homes, but, when the condition is diagnosed, her prolonged convalescence or hospitalization may necessitate special measures for their care elsewhere.

It is unnecessary here to rehearse the evidence pointing to unhappy childhood relationships being a major factor in the etiology of neurosis and to some extent also of psychosis. Some of the evidence relating these conditions to broken homes is reviewed in Appendix 1.[k]

Lack of parental control

In many countries legal machinery exists for removing children from their parents' care, either with or without parental consent, on the grounds of their being 'out of control'. Most of such children are neglected, maladjusted, or both. Since it is often a matter of chance under which designation a child is dealt with and since in any case maladjustment and lack of parental control are but the two sides of a single coin, no separate consideration will be given to this heading. Maladjustment is dealt with in chapter 14.

Unhappy marriage, desertion, separation, and divorce

Though a happy stable marriage is clearly a prerequisite for the effective family care of children, comparatively little research has been undertaken into factors contributing to it. The two most thorough inquiries were both carried out in the USA in the 1930s. Since in neither case was a psychiatrist or psycho-analyst engaged, there are no studies of the personalities and mental health of the couples. On the other hand, the conclusions regarding the influence of childhood factors are all the more striking as coming from an unexpected source.

Terman [138] conducted a statistical study of questionnaires completed by 792 couples in California. The three factors found to have the highest positive correlation with marital happiness were : marital happiness of the

---

k See page 161.

couples' parents ; happiness of childhood ; no conflict with mother. Naturally any study which relies on the questionnaire method and is dependent on the couples' reports is open to some doubts on the score of reliability. This is offset, however, by Burgess & Cottrell [36] reaching an almost identical conclusion from an independent inquiry. They also analysed questionnaires, in this case of 526 couples, mostly young middle-class Americans, in Illinois. From this part of their inquiry they conclude :

"The most significant association of any childhood familial factor with marital accord or discord established in this study is that of the reported happiness of the marriages of the parents of the husband and of the wife. Next in significance appear to be the closeness of attachment of the husband and the wife to their parents."

(For both wife and husband attachment to mother showed a higher positive correlation with marital happiness than that with father.) The identity of these findings with those of Terman is especially noted.

Burgess & Cottrell proceeded further, however, by adding to their statistical study a detailed clinical study of 100 couples. From this they conclude :

"The affectional relationships of childhood condition the love-life of the adult. The response patterns of relationships established in childhood appear to be the dynamic factor determining the expression of affection in adult life. This finding . . . corresponds more or less closely to the conclusions reached by other workers in their clinical analysis of material obtained over a prolonged period by intensive psychiatric interviews."

These conclusions arrived at independently by psychologists and sociologists of high standing must be taken as important confirmatory evidence of the main propositions underlying this report and of the particular proposition of this chapter—that deprived and unhappy children grow up to make bad parents.

Causes of Relatives Failing to Act as Substitutes

It has already been pointed out that it still remains the tradition in Western communities for near relatives to care for children when the natural home group has for any reason failed, and that no account of the causes of a particular child becoming homeless is complete unless the reason for relatives failing to act in this way is given. The usual reasons for failure are :

(a) Relatives dead, aged, or ill

(b) Relatives living far away

(c) Relatives unable to help for economic reasons

(d) Relatives unwilling to help

(e) The parents never had relatives (namely, were brought up in a series of foster-homes or an institution from early years).

It may well be that in present Western communities relatives are fewer, older, and less available for emergency aid than formerly owing to the combined effects of a lower birth-rate, higher age of marriage, the employment of women, and the fragmentation of society. Even so, there are probably few families which have no relatives and failure to help is likely often to be due to distance, lack of accommodation, or other economic difficulty. When this is so, judicious material aid could in many cases ensure that the child remained within his greater family group.

The conditions giving rise to most difficulty fall under heads (d) and (e) where relatives are either unwilling to help or have never been available.

Not infrequently the state of affairs which causes the failure of the parents to provide for the child is also the cause of relatives being unwilling to substitute. For instance, the unmarried mother not only has difficulties economically but may also be alienated from her relatives. The mental instability and psychopathy which frequently leads to poverty and neglect on the one hand, or to desertion on the other, is also likely to be associated with bad relations with relatives and neighbours. Brill, Children's Officer for Croydon, writes (personal communication) : " I always find out why the applicant cannot get help from relations and neighbours, and almost invariably it is because he himself is an unneighbourly person who has alienated the willingness of others to help." Personality factors may thus play an important part in destroying both the first and second line of defence against ' homelessness '.

Those who are fortunate to belong to large and united families are aware of the great sense of security they get from the knowledge that, should death suddenly overtake them, relatives willing to care for their children are certainly available. The absence of such a greater family is one of the many handicaps from which the child deprived of a normal home life suffers when he grows up and becomes a parent.

Though it is of the greatest importance to know the relative proportions of each of these five causes in a given community (since without such knowledge it is impossible to know in what fraction of cases better methods of work would permit the mobilization of relatives to help and in what fraction there is no alternative but community care) no studies appear to have been published.

* *
*

From the foregoing, it is evident that in a society where death-rates are low, the rate of employment high, and social welfare schemes adequate, it is emotional instability and the inability of parents to make effective family relationships which are the outstanding cause of children becoming deprived of a normal home life. This itself is an important conclusion, but it is perhaps even more important to note that the origin of adults being unable to make effective family relationships is not infrequently itself the result of their having been deprived of a normal home life in their own childhood. Thus the investigator is confronted with a self-perpetuating social circle in which children who are deprived of a normal home life grow up into parents unable to provide a normal home life for their children, thus leading to another generation of adults unable to do the same for theirs. Most workers in child care regard this vicious circle as playing an important part in the total problem. It is a matter which clearly requires much further investigation.

CHAPTER 9

PREVENTION OF FAMILY FAILURE

Since the basic method of preventing a child suffering maternal deprivation must be to ensure that he receives nurture within his own family, measures which promote this must be encouraged. On the probable success of such measures the League of Nations report of 1938 [90] is encouraging. After reviewing the resources available to a skilled case-worker, it concludes that " in the vast majority of cases, the careful use of such methods and resources ensures a quality of child care sufficient to meet the minimum requirements of the community and there is no need to remove the child from his own home " (volume 1, page 9). Such measures commonly comprise active assistance to the parents, economic, social, and medical.

Three objections are commonly lodged against a society making itself responsible for such action. The first is that of economy. Against this must be considered the immense cost to the community in ill-health, poor work, crime, and the breeding of further deprived children, all of which follow failure to take appropriate measures. The second objection is that providing parents with help undermines their initiative and self-reliance and makes them dependent. Such, of course, may follow if the help is given without enlisting the active participation of those helped. This, however, need not be. Skilled social workers have learnt to work *with* their clients, thereby developing their capacity for self-help. Only if the worker permits or encourages dependence by arbitrarily doing things for her clients, without their participation, need a dependent attitude result. Finally, there is the argument that the State should not intervene in family life. This raises broad issues, but it should be noted that just as children are absolutely dependent on their parents for sustenance, so in all but the most primitive communities are their parents, especially their mothers, dependent on a greater society for economic provision. If a community values its children it must cherish their parents.

Measures to prevent family failure are conveniently discussed under the three main headings which were recognized when considering its causes— economic, social, and medical. Since, however, any given measure frequently involves action under more than one of these it is preferable to fuse the three headings into two—socio-economic, and socio-medical. A further subdivision is useful—that between measures which may be applied immediately to a family in trouble and measures which have the long-term purpose of developing the community in such a way that family life is given the most favourable conditions in which to grow. There are thus the following four divisions :

Direct aid to families
    socio-economic
    socio-medical including psychiatric
Long-term community programmes
    socio-economic
    socio-medical including psychiatric.

Direct Aid to Families

Socio-economic aid

Although the League of Nations report [90] laid it down that

" it may therefore be regarded as an axiomatic principle of child care that no child should be removed from the care of an otherwise competent parent when the granting of material aid would make such removal unnecessary " (volume 1, page 8),

it is clear that this principle has yet to be acted upon in most countries. There are today governments prepared to spend the equivalent of up to 30 dollars a week on the residential care of infants who would tremble to give half this sum to a widow, an unmarried mother, or a grandmother to help her care for the baby at home. Indeed, nothing is more characteristic of both the public and voluntary attitude towards the problem than a willingness to spend large sums of money looking after children away from their homes, combined with a haggling parsimony in giving aid to the home itself. Many examples of this could be given, from the large sums spent to keep a child in hospital compared with the much smaller sums required to treat him at home, to the power of a British local authority to spend up to, say, £5 a week providing residence for a child, while being without the power to spend 30 shillings or so on bedding to enable him to live at home. Difficulties in regard to differential treatment of families there may be—if Mrs. Smith gets blankets why should not Mrs. Jones ?— but these difficulties must be solved by methods other than retaining the children in an institution.

In particular, far too little attention has been given to the needs of the home which has lost one parent only through death, illness, or other cause, a condition which characterizes about one quarter of all children in care ; clearly every effort must be made to help the other parent care for the children.

Husbandless mothers of children under five, and especially those under three who are still unfitted for nursery school or any form of community life, have the greatest difficulty in most countries in both making a living and caring for the children—activities which are incompatible when the children are very young. Though direct assistance to the mother is commonly meagre, in many cases public or voluntary funds are spent on the provision of day nurseries, which in parts of England, for instance, cost over £3 per head per week. This is not a fruitful way to spend the money, from the point of view either of health or of industrial production. As regards health, day-nurseries are known to have high rates of infectious illness and are believed to have an adverse effect on the children's emotional growth. As regards production, there is little net gain in woman-power, since for every 100 mothers employed 50 workers are necessary to care for the babies and, as every industrialist knows, mothers of young children are unsatisfactory employees and often absent on account of minor illnesses at home. For these reasons day care as a means of helping the husbandless mother should be restricted to children over three who are able to adapt to nursery school. Until the child has reached this age, direct economic assistance should be given to the mother.

In the case of fathers who are left with motherless children, either temporarily while the mother is in hospital or permanently, the provision of a housekeeper service is much preferable to removing the children. This service, which has been developed by agencies in Canada and the USA, is described by Baylor & Monachesi : [12]

" The time given by the housekeepers varies from two hours a day to resident service, but in several instances the housekeeper has continued with one family for several years. Before housekeeper service is given, the agency requires that the family shall have one reliable member, usually a father or an older child . . . It has been said that house-keepers are ' foster mothers in reverse '. In the case of a foster mother youth is an asset, but with a housekeeper it is a liability. Another striking difference is that while the foster mother spends her own money, the housekeeper spends another person's money . . .

" The advantages arising from the housekeeper service have been summarized by the Protestant Children's Home of Toronto as follows :

" Holds the father's interest and sense of responsibility.

" Gives the children more security in their family relationships.

" By preserving the home and equipment it avoids the prolonged break-up which generally results from boarding-home placement no matter how devoted the father may be.

" Less expensive than boarding care in large families.

" More normal relationship and status for a child in the community than if he is in a boarding home.

" Avoids the real tragedy that occurs when a child grows into a boarding-home family and has to be uprooted " (pages 38, 39).

It will be observed that, at least with large families, this method of care is actually cheaper than removing the children, yet, apart from the home-help schemes in Britain and Sweden, it does not seem to be common in European countries at present.

On grounds of financial economy as well as the child's mental health, then, it is to be hoped that governments and voluntary agencies alike will, before allocating further funds for the care of children away from their homes, consider whether everything possible has been done financially to assist parents to care for them at home. Spence [131] puts the matter pithily when he remarks : " Much that passes for social aid to mothers is construed in a way which raises their fears and undermines their confidence. They are relieved of their children when they should be relieved of their chores " (page 50).

Socio-medical aid

Essential though socio-economic aid frequently is, it is often useless unless help of a socio-medical kind is given as well. In many cases there would be no economic problem at all were it not for physical or mental illness, psychopathic character, or conflict in the home.

Although the provision of services for the care of the physical health of parents, especially the mothers of young children, is of the utmost importance, this has now become accepted practice in many Western countries and so need not detain us here. A special service which has not yet received the recognition which it deserves is the provision of rest homes to which mothers may go with their younger children. Such a home has been established near Manchester, England, since the end of the late war, and is described at some length in the report of Mrs. Hubback's group.[110] To this home, a mother who is either in physical ill-health or on the verge of a mental breakdown may go for weeks or months to recuperate, without the problems of having to arrange for the younger children's care or the anxiety of wondering how they are faring—an anxiety both inevitable and proper for the mother of small children. Moreover, if such a home is run with insight into the emotional problems of mothers and children, much quiet help can be given to the mothers to establish a relationship of security and mutual affection on which, as has been seen, the child's future mental health depends.

Another service which is only as yet in an embryo stage in most countries is that of marriage guidance. Before effective measures to help married couples who are in difficulties can be devised, there must be a sound understanding of the causes of marriage failure. In several countries there has been considerable emphasis laid on ignorance of the physical side of marriage and of sex technique, but most with experience now realize that this is only a small—and an easily remedied—part of the problem. Far more important are the personalities of the partners. Burgess & Cottrell,[36] it will be remembered, concluded as a result of their inquiry that " the affectional relationships of childhood condition the love-life of the adult ", and it is this basic truth which underlies modern techniques. Berkowitz,[54] in his contribution to a useful symposium by American social workers on the diagnosis and treatment of marital problems, remarks : " We see that people who come to us because of marriage difficulty have carried over unresolved childhood problems into the marriage to an extensive degree." Unless these are clearly recognized and attention given to them, little progress in better adaptation can be effected. In particular, it is necessary for the social worker to be aware both of the strong unconscious drives which lead husbands and wives to create the very problems of which they complain and of the distorted light in which they see the behaviour of their spouse. Not only may husbands and wives provoke a marriage partner to unkind behaviour, but they may genuinely believe that their behaviour is far worse than it really is. The difficulties are thus the diffi- culties of one or both partners in making satisfactory human relationships and as such are to be understood in psychiatric and psycho-analytic terms.

Although these personality difficulties stemming from childhood must be counted as the most frequent and weighty factors in marital maladjust- ment, faults in the social matrix within which the couple live must not be overlooked. Reference has already been made to the social fragmentation which characterizes many Western communities of the present day and this, as Wilson [149] points out, is apt to force husbands and wives

" to seek within the family the satisfaction of personal and social needs which are by their nature impossible to satisfy there. In these circumstances the family ties are, as it were, carrying an amount of ' current ' for which they were not designed, and it is not surprising that what corresponds to ' fusing ' is a not infrequent occurrence."

Marriage guidance to be effective must therefore take account of both broad sociological factors and internal psychological ones. The practi- tioner must be trained to see the particular marital problem presented as but a symptom of a socio-psychological maladjustment, and to treat not the symptom but the pathological processes lying behind it.

The same considerations apply when there is friction between parents and children, a not infrequent cause of children being removed from home. The particular problem—bedwetting, stealing, aggressiveness, or whatever it may be—is to be conceived as merely the presenting symptom in a far more complex and often partially hidden situation in which the psycho- pathology of the parents usually plays a major part. Child-guidance workers clearly recognize this and, despite the name, nowadays give as much time to the therapy of the parents as to that of the children. It is true that at one time child-guidance services themselves were all too fre- quently the cause of children being removed from home, but the leading clinics in Europe and America no longer look on the removal of the child from home as a wise step. Naturally there are cases where a temporary change may be of value, and others where the child's home is unmendable, such as, for instance, when the mother is a prostitute. However, greater understanding of the psychodynamics of family relations, combined with greater technical skill in handling them, have gone far to change policy in the direction of mending the home instead of disrupting it. Many seemingly intractable problems when approached with insight and skill are found to be treatable, since there is in almost all families a tremendous need to live together in greater accord, and this provides a powerful motive for favourable change. It is the task of the therapist, whether medical or not, to help provide conditions in which this drive can re-assert itself so that, though all may not be perfect, the essential features of a good home are restored. The provision of child-guidance services on a generous scale must therefore be regarded as a major contribution to the maintenance of family life and so to the promotion of mental health. Furthermore, it is now agreed that work of this kind is of particular value in the case of young children and their mothers, since it is in the first few years of life that the pattern of later parent-child relationships is laid down. The troubles of adolescents are no more than the reverberations of conflicts which began in these early years. Difficulties which are insoluble at 13 may be handled quickly and effectively at three. It is by giving priority to work in these early years that our best hope of prevention lies.

Special educational arrangements for maladjusted children are also of value. Since 1939, the City of Amsterdam has provided one or two specially staffed day-schools to which children are referred by its mental health division after thorough psychiatric investigation and diagnosis. There is close contact between teachers and psychiatrists, and special efforts are made to work with the children's parents and to arrange vocational guidance and after-care. More recently the County of London has followed Amsterdam's lead.

In the case of older children—eight years and over—the use of expedients such as boarding-schools may be of value. If the child is maladjusted, it may be useful for him to be away for part of the year from the tensions which produced his difficulties, and if the home is bad in other ways the same is true. The boarding-school has the great advantage of preserving the child's all-important home ties, even if in slightly attenuated form, and, since it forms a part of the ordinary social pattern of most Western communities today, the child who goes to boarding-school will not feel different from other children. Moreover, by relieving the parents of the children for part of the year, it will be possible for some of them to develop more favourable attitudes towards their children during the remainder.

Finally, there is the question of problem families. Querido [118] has divided them into three groups :

(a) those which, provided economic and medical help can be given, can become once again effective social units ;

(b) those which may require some degree of permanent help but which can respond favourably to it ;

(c) those which all ordinary social measures are powerless to assist.

The work required for the rehabilitation of the first two groups has been well described in the report of Mrs. Hubback's committee.[110] Experience has shown that the combination of insight into causes, sympathetic contact, and hard manual work, with medical and financial aid, can save many homes which in other hands would have involved moral condemnation and no social action but their destruction. Such help is of particular value where ignorance, poverty, and physical ill-health have been the causes of the family failure. Where temperamental instability or psychopathy of the parents is the root cause, such measures commonly fail, and for this reason workers need psychiatric insight if they are to avoid breaking their hearts on cases they cannot help.

There is as yet no agreed plan for tackling families where failure is due to parental psychopathy. Probably the most realistic and constructive proposal at present under discussion is that of Querido for placing whole families under supervision and restraint by providing for them special units each of which could accommodate a small number of problem families and which would be the responsibility of trained workers. He argues that, just as it is regarded as necessary for the sake of their own well-being and the well-being of others to place under supervision individuals who are mentally ill, so is it reasonable to place under supervision psychopathic families which are endangering the well-being of their own members and others. A programme of this kind would in almost all countries require legislation and this is now being drafted in the Netherlands. Querido has recognized that his proposal " involves a serious infringement of personal liberty and offers possibilities of abuse " but, as he himself emphasizes, problem families constitute a very serious and self-perpetuating danger to social progress. Until more effective measures for rehabilitating psycho-pathic characters can be found or until long-term measures of mental hygiene have proved successful in preventing their development, this indeed may be the right solution.

Long-Term Community Programmes

Socio-economic developments

The fragmentation of society in Western industrialized communities and the break-up of the greater family pose grave problems. To discuss how these basic social trends should be reversed or their effects on family life mitigated is outside the scope of this report. Nevertheless, a comprehensive policy for the prevention of children becoming ' deprived ' cannot afford to ignore them, and in this field the less-developed communities may well have much to offer the more-developed ones. One point should be noted —the great economic vulnerability of the family with children. Beveridge has reported that in England " a family still remains the greatest single cause of poverty ", a condition which clearly holds true elsewhere in the Western world. This has led in many countries to the provision of family allowances, a vital step in the right direction. Even so, it must be considered whether some specially increased provision should not be made for children under five or three. It has been seen that it is at this age that they are at their most dependent and from a mental health point of view at their most vulnerable. The mother of young children is far more tied than is the mother of school-age children, for whom part-time work is quite possible. Since the mother of young children is not free, or at least should not be free, to earn, there is a strong argument for increased family allowances for children in these early years.

Socio-medical developments

An additional reason for adequate and graded family allowances is that poverty, with resultant overwork and under-nourishment, is a potent cause of parental ill-health, both physical and to a lesser degree mental, and this, as has been seen, is a major cause of children becoming deprived. But even if the basis of preventive health is an equitable social and economic system, personal health services have much to contribute. Here again parents, and especially mothers of young children, must have priority if family failure is to be avoided.

A special word is appropriate here on the need for long-term programmes of mental hygiene. Hitherto, these have been difficult to plan because of a lack of agreement regarding the origins of mental ill-health. For long it has been known that certain relatively rare conditions are caused by infection and that a few others are inherited. The vast majority of cases, however, comprising all the neuroses and so-called personality disturbances have remained a mystery and the source of controversy. This is now changing as evidence accumulates pointing to the child's experience in his family in his early years as being of central importance for his healthy emotional development. The outstanding disability of persons suffering from mental illness, it is now realized, is their inability to make and sustain confident, friendly, and co-operative relations with others. The potential ability to do this is as basic to man's nature as are the abilities to see or digest, and, just as we regard failing vision or indigestion as signs of ill-health and the results of trauma, so have we now come to regard the inability to make reasonably co-operative human relations. The growth of this ability, as has been seen, is determined in very high degree by the quality of the child's relation to his parents in his early years. It is on the basis of this theory of etiology that the report of the Expert Committee on Mental Health of the World Health Organization on its first session [157] emphasized " the desirability of concentrating especially on the therapeutic and preventive psychiatry of childhood ".

In practice, this means not only treating children but the giving of psychiatric help to parents, especially the parents of very young children, who are in a plastic phase of emotional development and who therefore respond rapidly. Since the need for psychotherapy vastly outstrips its supply and an order of priority is unavoidable if rational use is to be made of what exists, pride of place must go to patients who are both of key importance and respond in a quick and lasting way. Those who have worked with the parents, especially the mothers, of young children believe that there is no more fruitful mental hygiene work than this.

In addition, preventive mental hygiene demands early and effective aid to families who have already got into difficulties, including measures to avoid the removal of children from home, and, finally, the best possible provision for children who for any reason cannot remain at home. By such measures it may, in the course of two or three generations, be possible to enable all boys and girls to grow up to become men and women who, given health and economic security, are capable of providing a stable and happy family life for their children. In this way, it may be hoped both to promote mental health and to eliminate very many of the factors which at present cause children to be deprived of maternal care.

The long-term programme of mental hygiene is thus seen to be the psychiatric care of individual families writ large.

This programme for the prevention of family failure, it is recognized, demands great effort. That part of it primarily concerned with social and psychological services, such as marriage guidance, child guidance, and work with the parents of very young children, requires large numbers of skilled workers. Their training and maintenance will take time and money, but is likely in the long run to be a far cheaper and more efficient method of solving the problem of ' homeless children ' than the mere provision of foster-homes and institutions.

One question which is likely to be asked is in regard to the position in this programme of professional personnel without a psychiatric training—physicians, nurses, social workers, and others. Are they to be excluded from participating ? On the contrary, the answer is simple and clear : only if all these workers are trained can the work be done on the necessary scale. The stage has been reached in preventive medicine in Western countries where disorders springing from infection and malnutrition are, to a large extent, conquered and where health workers are free to give time and energy to mental health. This is admirable, but, before these workers can be effective, extensive retraining and radical changes in outlook and attitude will be necessary. The principles and practice of psychological medicine and preventive mental health cannot be learnt in a few weeks or even a few months any more easily than can the principles and practice of physical medicine and preventive physical health be learnt in this time. Unless the amount of training and change of attitude which are required are clearly recognized and tackled, the devolution of this work to the non-specialist will prove abortive. All those aspiring to work in this field must become thoroughly familiar with the psychology and psychopathology of human relations, alive to unconscious motivation, and able to modify it. Such widespread professional training and retraining is today the foremost need both in mental hygiene and the preservation of the family.

CHAPTER 10

ILLEGITIMACY AND DEPRIVATION

In Western communities two types of illegitimacy are distinguishable, the first of which is socially accepted and the second of which is socially not accepted. Among the illegitimacy which is relatively accepted in certain Western communities can be placed the convention that, before it is wise to marry her, the girl should demonstrate her fecundity. Another example is the convention for a couple to live together as though married despite not having gone through a legal ceremony. Finally, there are sub-cultures, usually among the poorer classes, where the possession of an illegitimate child is not held against the mother and both are given support within the greater family.

Unfortunately, official statistics relating to illegitimacy do not make this vital distinction and are consequently of little use. From the point of view of the prevention of children growing up deprived of a normal home life, it is imperative to have accurate figures showing the rates of illegitimacy of the socially unacceptable kind, since it is only these children who are at risk. This report will be concerned only with such cases.

Character and Home Background of Parents of Illegitimate Children

Until recently, the fact that some girls become pregnant illicitly was looked upon somewhat fatalistically and dismissed as just human nature. Apart from moral exhortation, little attention was given to prevention. Studies carried out in America make clear, however, that the girl who has a socially unacceptable illegitimate baby often comes from an unsatisfactory family background and has developed a neurotic character, the illegitimate baby being in the nature of a symptom of her neurosis.

Young,[158] for instance, carried out a study of 100 unmarried mothers between the ages of 18 and 40, who, although representing wide variations in intelligence, education, and social and economic backgrounds, were if anything rather above average in intelligence. She found that 48 of these girls had dominating and rejecting mothers and another 20 had dominating and rejecting fathers, and that the girl's relation to the dominant parent " was a battleground on which a struggle was fought, and the baby was an integral part of that struggle ". No fewer than 43 of the 100 girls had been brought up in broken homes, a finding confirmed by a Toronto study [142] which gives a figure of 30 broken homes in the histories of 57 unmarried mothers, and a further 10 with quarrelling parents. All the girls studied by Young had grown up to have

" fundamental problems in their relationships with other people. Some of them could not carry on even superficial contacts successfully ; others did well with casual acquaintances and friends but were unable to enter into a close or intimate relationship with anyone . . . The problems followed them into their work and few of them were able to use more than a small part of their native intelligence and ability . . . All these girls, unhappy and driven by unconscious needs, had blindly sought a way out of their emotional dilemma by having an out-of-wedlock child. It is not strange that one finds among them almost no girl who has genuinely cared for or been happy with the father of her baby."

Practically none of these girls was promiscuous and only one-quarter of the group had had more than a fleeting relationship with the father of the child. In all of them there appeared a strong unconscious desire to become pregnant, motivated sometimes by the need for a love-object which they had never had and sometimes by the desire to use the shame of an illegitimate baby as a weapon against their dominating parents. It was noteworthy that a large group insisted in a rigid and irrational way on their mother looking after the baby, despite her objections. Running side by side with the need to use the baby as a weapon against the parents was the need to use it as a weapon against themselves.

" One of the most frequent tendencies to be found in their personality patterns was that of self-punishment. Almost none of the cases was completely free of it and with many of them it represented the major force in their lives. So deeply ingrained and so powerful was this force that often the girl would permit nothing and nobody to interfere with its self-destructive progress."

Though it is impossible to know how typical Young's findings are, it is the opinion of many social workers with psychiatric knowledge and experience of this problem that with many girls becoming an unmarried mother is neurotic and not just accidental. In other cases the girls are psychopathic or defective. For instance, of 93 unmarried mothers whose children were in the care of Dr. Barnardo's Homes,[110] 25 are described as moral defectives, and were no doubt promiscuous, a further 10 were dull and backward, mentally defective, or insane. No particulars are given regarding the others, though some, no doubt, were similar in character to those described by Young.

The character of the unmarried father is rarely studied and not much is known of him. It is the opinion of experienced social workers that many are unstable and that they often promise marriage irresponsibly. Compared to the unmarried mother, they are more often promiscuous and get several girls into trouble within a short time. The psychology of habitually promiscuous men has been studied in connexion with the prevention of venereal disease. Wittkower,[152] after studying 200 soldiers suffering from this disease and a control group numbering 861 matched for age, army service, and location, suffering from impetigo, concluded :

" The all-round picture which emerges is that venereal disease patients are often emotionally, sexually, and socially immature, whereas physically and intellectually they may have reached full maturity. As may be expected, evidence of immaturity is more striking in habitually promiscuous than in occasionally promiscuous individuals . . . Fifty-nine per cent. of our venereal disease patients, against 19% in the control series, were found to be emotionally immature. Only 11% of the venereal disease patients, as compared with 62% in the control series, could be regarded as mature personalities."

Among factors which make for promiscuity, Wittkower lists the need for affection, situations which arouse anxiety, and situations which arouse resentment. " The so-called biological sex-urge, strange though it may appear, plays a minor part in most cases of promiscuity ", in the same way that thirst has little to do with chronic alcoholism.

In seeking to understand the origins of these unstable, immature characters, whose antisocial behaviour brings so much misery in its train, one is led back, as in the case of many of the unmarried mothers, to their childhoods and their relationships with their own parents. Abstracts of two studies relating promiscuity to broken homes are given in Appendix 1,[1] but for completeness sake are repeated here. In their study of 255 promiscuous males, Safier et al.[127] discovered that 60% came from homes which had been broken by death, separation, or divorce, the average age of the child when the home broke up being six years.

" Among the patients whose homes had been broken, it was not unusual for the patient to have been placed in boarding schools, foster homes, institutions, or in the homes of relatives. A number of the patients had had a series of such placements. Some patients had had no care by either parent from birth or shortly thereafter. Some of those had been born out of wedlock. In other instances one or both parents had remarried and the patients were reared in homes with stepfathers or stepmothers. The patients reported difficulties in adjusting to successive changes in the family pattern. Inconsistencies in training and discipline were frequently the result of constant shifting from the care of one parent to that of another . . . Conflicts were most pronounced in the cases where the family life had been unstable and the patient had been entrusted to the care of first one person and then another " (page 10).

This picture is confirmed by Bundesen et al.[35] who, with a group of 50 similar patients, found evidence of abnormal childhood conditions leading to a broken home in 56%.

Preliminary studies such as these go far to demonstrate that, in a Western community, it is emotionally disturbed men and women who produce illegitimate children of a socially unacceptable kind. Moreover, they give further prominence to the social process already emphasized as being of the greatest consequence for the production of children who will grow up deprived of maternal care—the process whereby one generation of deprived children provides the parents of the next generation of deprived children.

Care of Illegitimates

There are two ways of approaching the problem of preventing the illegitimate child becoming in need of care away from home—to prevent his

[1] See page 161.

being conceived and to make realistic plans for his care if he is. The reduction of the birth-rate of socially unacceptable illegitimates is a matter for long-term measures of mental hygiene which are discussed later. Meanwhile it seems likely that for many decades to come Western communities will have to face the problem of how best to care for such children. Though it is evident that in this, as in all problems, the most effective measures are possible only if there is real knowledge and understanding, the absence of studies on how illegitimates may best be cared for is conspicuous.

In several countries of Europe, e.g., the Netherlands, Sweden, and the United Kingdom, policy is strongly in favour of the unmarried mother keeping her child. For instance, in a circular issued by the British Ministry of Health,[74] the duties of a social worker in helping the unmarried mother are stated as, first, " whenever possible to persuade the girl to make known her circumstances to her parents and, if the home is likely to be a satisfactory one, to persuade the grandparents to make a home there for the little one ", to continue by considering alternatives such as residential employment, day nurseries, foster-homes, or residential nurseries, and only " in special cases, e.g., where the mother is very young or is the wife of a man not the father of the child, to give advice about legal adoption ". In the Netherlands adoption is not legal. Yet when one inquires in these countries for studies of how the illegitimate child who is not adopted actually fares, none seems to be available. Reports such as that of the Medical Officer of Health for Willesden [148] are far from reassuring, however. In a very disturbing account of the hazardous and ever-changing lives of foster-children in the borough in 1939, he writes :

" The majority of foster children are illegitimate. Their mothers are frequently in employment and may work up to a month before confinement. During this last month when they are not employed they must keep themselves and make some provision for the child. They are generally confined in hospital. At the end of ten days or a fortnight they are discharged. They have no money left. They have nowhere to go. They are handicapped by the child. It is important that they get work at once. What often happens seems to be that such a mother finds some woman who, perhaps out of kindness or perhaps in hope of money later on, takes the child whilst the mother searches for work. The child may be well cared for or not, but in any case the mother probably in the circumstances does not inquire too closely. She is glad to get anybody to take the child. If she gets work and pays the woman it may be that the child stays on for a time but if the payments are small and irregular the child may be passed from one woman to another, finding no stability in life at all."

There is no reason to suppose the position in Great Britain to have changed in the past decade. One London agency concerned with the care of unmarried mothers, reporting on the placement of over 1,000 babies in the period 1949-1950, shows that 22% were placed with foster-parents or in a residential nursery soon after birth. Only 17% were adopted. The bulk of the remainder were living with their unmarried mothers. That many of these will sooner or later also find their way into foster-homes or nurseries is indicated by another London agency which, stating that it is its policy in all suitable cases to encourage unmarried mothers to keep the custody of their children and to give the mothers, when necessary, financial and other assistance to make it possible, proceeds : " It has to be faced however that lack of accommodation makes it increasingly difficult for an unmarried mother to have her baby with her continually from its birth, and during some considerable part of its childhood it is more than likely to be fostered or placed in a residential nursery " (personal communications).

The absence of satisfactory figures for any country of Western Europe is a measure of their neglect of this problem, while such information as is available makes it clear that in some countries at least a large fraction of illegitimates, perhaps more than half, under the present haphazard arrangements grow up suffering from some degree of maternal deprivation and into characters likely to produce more of their kind. The absence of studies of the later development of unmarried mothers (despite strong opinions being expressed about this or that course being in their best interests) is also symptomatic of the absence both of public concern and of a scientific approach to the problem.

The picture in Canada and the USA is rather different. In the last decade there have been a few studies of what has actually happened to illegitimates who have not been adopted. In 1943, the Welfare Council of Toronto and District [142] published a study of the history and adjustment of illegitimate children aged 14 and 15 years who had remained with their mothers or relatives. Of the 92 children studied (49 boys, 43 girls) only 25 had remained with the same family group since birth, though a further 19 had been accompanied by their mothers through a variety of changing circumstances. The remaining 48 (52%) had changed their mother-figures —usually two, three, or more times. The study goes further, however, in that it demonstrates first that a large proportion of these children (47%) are showing signs of maladjustment and secondly that this is related to their experiences. This is shown clearly in table XII, which relates the

TABLE XII. INCIDENCE OF MALADJUSTMENT RELATED TO AGE AT WHICH ILLEGITIMATE CHILD IS PERMANENTLY SETTLED (TORONTO STUDY)

Adjustment of child	Age in years by which settled			Total
	before 3	4-7	after 7	
	%	%	%	%
Maladjusted	33	50	84	47
Adjusted	67	50	16	53
	100	100	100	100
Number of children . . .	55	18	19	92

Note : P is less than .01.

incidence of maladjustment to the age at which the child became a permanent member of a family group.

From this it is evident that the earlier the child is settled the better—hardly a surprising conclusion. In 21 cases (17 boys, 4 girls) their maladjustment took the form of delinquency, mostly stealing and truancy. One girl of 15 had already run away and become pregnant—another example of the vicious circle of the deprived reproducing themselves. How many of the other 20 delinquents—nearly one-quarter of the whole group—will grow up to produce illegitimate or deprived children ?

The report states that with few exceptions the homes from which the delinquents came were unstable and unhappy. " Children were taken out of homes where they were happy and thought they belonged into homes where they were not wanted. Others have been rejected practically since birth by the people with whom they lived." Here is more evidence, if it is still needed, that deprivation causes maladjustment.

The Toronto inquiry reveals a sorry state of affairs, which its authors relate directly to the policy pursued by the agencies advising these unmarried mothers at the time of the children's births—that the unmarried mother should look after her own baby. It was clear that this rather rigid policy had over-influenced many of the mothers, some of whom having cared for their babies during the period of greatest dependency found it impossible to release them later, even when they learned that the future offered little opportunity for satisfactory living for themselves and little chance of normal growth for their children. Others had quickly rebelled against the agencies' rulings and had got rid of their children as best they could. In other cases again the mother's parents had been forced, urged, or encouraged to provide homes, despite the relationship between the mother and her parents having for long been unhappy, with the result that the baby became the cause of yet further friction. Naturally there were cases where the arrangement of the mother or her parents looking after the baby had worked well, but this seems to have occurred only when the mother was stable, had good relations with her parents, and was fond of the baby and his father—not a very frequent set of circumstances.

A little earlier, in New York, Rome [125] had studied 30 mothers who had committed their illegitimate babies to an institution pending a final decision, and had come to a similar conclusion. Of the 30, only 8 were finally taken home by their mothers, 4 were adopted and, after a lapse of three years, 15 remained in the institution or in foster-homes. But not only does she demonstrate that, after three years, half these mothers were still unable to come to a long-term decision, but she points to the fact that the outcome could with a high degree of certainty have been predicted from the time of the baby's birth. Only if at least four of the following conditions are present is the mother likely to take the baby home : that she is of stable personality, takes a realistic attitude towards her problem, is loving and accepting of the child, had a positive relation to the putative father, and has a family which docs not insist on the child being disposed of. If Young's findings regarding the psychology of unmarried mothers are typical, and the Toronto study suggests that they may be, it will be seen that such conditions are present in only a minority of cases.

Of the group of children whose mothers neither relinquish nor take responsibility for them, Embry [53] has written :

" The child continues in an institution or foster home, or more likely a series of foster homes, a tragic example of nobody's child. The mother visits occasionally. She may bring him presents. Rarely she pays a little for his board. When asked about plans for him she always reiterates that some day she will take him, but that some day never seems to come. By the time the agency is convinced of the need for an enforced surrender, the child has probably grown beyond the age when he can be easily placed for adoption."

In a booklet published by the Children's Bureau of the US Department of Labor, Morlock [105] gives an illustration :

" One such child at 10 years of age is a disturbed, bewildered boy with many behavior problems. He has lived in 20 foster homes. At the time of his birth his mother was a docile, receptive girl who agreed with the philosophy of the maternity home that she should keep her baby. Her parents refused to allow her to live at home if she kept him. She went to work in a store, paid the child's board regularly, and visited him in the foster home every 2 weeks. Gradually, however, her payments stopped. Twice she attempted suicide. Either the original plan was an unsuitable one for both her and the child, or the mother was not given enough case-work assistance in carrying out the plan " (page 28).

As a result of data such as these, progressive policy in the USA in regard to illegitimates has changed abruptly in the last ten years and far more adoptions are being arranged. Social workers now conceive it to be their duty to help the unmarried mother face the real situation before her, which so often is that of an immature girl, on bad terms with her family, with no financial security, having to undertake with little or no help the care of an infant for whom she has mixed feelings, over a period of many years. If this is in fact the real situation and it is put before her in a sympathetic way by someone whom she has learned to trust, the majority of girls recognize that it is in the interest of neither themselves nor the baby to attempt to care for him, and are prepared to release him for adoption. As a valuable paper by Young [159] and the booklet by Morlock & Campbell [105] go to show, American social workers have become self-critical of their previous inclination to avoid responsibility for making a long-term plan and for unwittingly helping the unmarried mother herself to evade it. For this is in fact what voluntary and public agencies are doing when they receive illegitimate children into care without insisting that the mothers either make realistic long-term plans to provide care themselves, or else permit others to do so—by arranging adoption. In some countries, e.g., Great Britain, the law is such that authorities have no option but to accede to the mother's temporizing measures, compelling them to care for the child while at the same time permitting the mother indefinitely to refuse consent for adoption. In framing laws of this kind, the paramount consideration is clearly the parents' right to the possession of the child, the child's welfare taking second place.

Unfortunately, instead of considering objectively what is best for the child and what is best for the mother, workers of all kinds have too often been influenced by punitive or sentimental attitudes towards the errant mother. At one time the punitive attitude took the form of removing the baby from his mother as a punishment for her sins. Nowadays this punitive attitude seems to lead in the opposite direction and to insist that she should take the responsibility for caring for what she has so irresponsibly produced. In a similar way, sentimentalism can lead to either conclusion. Only by getting away from these irrational attitudes and preparing to study the problem afresh is a realistic set of working principles likely to be adopted. It is urgently necessary in many countries to make studies of what in fact happens to the illegitimate children of today—how many achieve a satisfactory home life with their mothers or immediate relatives, how many eke out their existence in foster-homes or institutions, and how many are adopted and what is the outcome. Furthermore, it is necessary to study the development of the unmarried mother and to devise means of helping her avoid such tangles in the future and to achieve a more satisfactory way of life. It may perhaps be that, in some cases, encouraging her to take the responsibility for her baby will help her become a more responsible citizen, but to act on the assumption that this is always the case is not only to be unrealistic but to be socially irresponsible ourselves. For it is a very serious thing to condemn a child to be parked in an endless succession of foster-homes or to be brought up in an institution when there are long waiting lists of suitable parents wishing to adopt children.

Hitherto most nations have preferred to forget the existence of illegitimate children or, in so far as they have aided them, it has been too little and too late. If a community is to remove this source of deprived children, it will have to be more realistic in its handling of the problem, both by providing economic and psychological assistance to the unmarried mother to enable her to care for her child and by providing skilled services to arrange for the adoption of those children who cannot be so cared for.

CHAPTER 11

SUBSTITUTE FAMILIES. I : ADOPTION

" The central paradox of work for deprived children is that there are thousands of childless homes crying out for children and hundreds of Homes filled with children in need of family life." This situation, graphically described in the annual report of the Children's Officer of an English borough,[47] obtains in many Western countries. Yet very little serious study has been given to the problems of adoption, and it is only gradually becoming recognized as a process requiring scientific understanding and professional skill. Too often the baby's future is the concern only of a well-meaning amateur or of a health visitor trained to consider no more than physical hygiene. Once again scientific studies of the subject are conspicuous by their scarcity.

The process of adoption concerns three sets of people—the mother, the baby (almost always illegitimate), and the prospective adopters. There is skilled work to be done with each. First, help must be given to the mother to enable her to reach a realistic decision ; this requires skill in making a relationship of mutual confidence with her, in understanding her personality and her social situation, and in helping her face unpalatable facts in a constructive way. Secondly, there must be an ability to assess the potentialities of the baby—no easy task and one about which there are many ungrounded assumptions. Finally, there must be an ability to predict how a couple will care for children, often in the absence of any direct demonstration of their capacities, and to help them in the initial adjustments. These are formidable tasks. Furthermore, they must be discharged reasonably quickly since all with experience are agreed that the baby should be adopted as early in his life as possible.

The evidence given in Part I of this report points unmistakably to its being in the interests of the adopted baby's mental health for him to be adopted soon after birth. No other arrangement permits continuity of mothering and most other arrangements fail even to ensure its adequacy. If the baby remains with his mother, it is not unlikely that she will neglect and reject him. The work of Rheingold and Levy has shown that if he is parked temporarily in a nursery or group foster-home his development will often suffer in some degree (see page 18). Nothing is more tragic than good adoptive parents who accept for adoption a child whose early experiences have led to disturbed personality development which nothing they can now do will rectify. Very early adoption is thus clearly in the interests also of the adoptive parents. Moreover, the nearer to birth that they have had him the more will they feel the baby to be their own and the easier will it be for them to identify themselves with his personality. Favourable relationships will then have the best chance to develop.

The arguments against very early adoption are three in number :

(a) it requires what might be a precipitate decision by the mother

(b) the baby cannot be breast fed

(c) there is less opportunity to assess the baby's potential development.

Of these the first argument is the most weighty. It is clearly of the greatest importance not only that the right decision should be reached by the mother but that it should be reached by her in a way which leaves her convinced that she has decided wisely. This may take time, though, as Rome has shown, no good comes from prolonging the period of indecision indefinitely. If the mother has sought care reasonably early it should be possible for the experienced case-worker to help her reach a realistic decision either before the baby is born or soon after, since most of the factors which matter (e.g., stability of personality, realism towards the problem, and attitude towards the putative father) will be evident in her life before the birth of the baby. If all of these are adverse the baby's birth will not change them, and the likelihood is small of the mother making a success of looking after the child. More knowledge, skill, and realism on the part of case-workers could undoubtedly lead to wise and emotionally satisfactory decisions being reached fairly early in a large proportion of cases.

Moreover, it is in the mother's interest to make the decision to keep or part with her baby early rather than late. Unless it is reasonably clear that she will be able to care for the child, it is no kindness to permit her to become attached to him ; parting is then all the more heart-breaking. Some unmarried mothers decide, after reflection, that they would prefer not to see their baby, a decision which should be respected. Rigid policies that all unmarried mothers must care for their babies for three or six months and must breast feed them can have no place in a service designed to help illegitimate babies and their unmarried mothers to live happy and useful lives.

It is, of course, only when a baby is likely to be breast fed that the interruption of breast-feeding is an argument against early adoption, since if the mother is averse to such feeding or if the baby is to be deposited in a nursery or foster-home the matter becomes irrelevant. If early adoption does in fact mean depriving a baby of breast-feeding it is, of course, a serious matter. Even so, to reach the correct decision regarding the best age for the child to be adopted requires the weighing of one set of medical disadvantages against another and only far more research than has been done into the adverse effects of each can permit the decision to be realistic. Meanwhile, it is unwise to assume that breast-feeding and later adoption is better for the baby's future welfare than early adoption and affectionate artificial feeding.

The third argument against early adoption—that there is less opportunity to assess the baby's potential development—is commonly used by psychologists but is the weakest of the three. It rests on the assumption that the various tests of development available in the first year of life have predictive value for the child's later mental development. In an exhaustive inquiry Bayley [11] has shown that this assumption is not justified. She shows that the correlation of test performance at nine months of age with that at four years is zero and that " scores made before eighteen months are completely useless in the prediction of school-age abilities ". This same conclusion is reached by Michaels & Brenner [103] in one of the comparatively few pieces of systematic research on adoption. They carried out a follow-up of 50 adopted children when they were four years of age or over both to discover what proportion had proved successful and what were the most reliable criteria for making predictions. They conclude rather sadly that " the psychologist's findings, in this and other studies, suggest that the case-worker's tendency to assume that infant tests provide a safe index of potential development is not warranted ".[m] Not only is this so but, as has been seen, there is a very serious danger that keeping a baby in a nursery awaiting adoption in the belief that in a few more months an accurate prediction can be made will itself produce retardation, which is then taken as evidence that the baby is inherently backward. Hence there develops the paradoxical situation in which misguided caution in arranging adoption creates a baby which at first appears, and ultimately becomes, unfitted for it.

Probably the best guide to potential intelligence is the intelligence of the parents, though for many reasons this can be no more than a very rough guide and adoptive parents like natural parents must be prepared to take a normal biological risk.

It will be seen, therefore, that the arguments against early adoption are far less strong than they appear at first sight. On psychiatric and social grounds adoption in the first two months should become the rule, though some flexibility will always be necessary to permit mothers to work their way to a satisfactory decision. If during the waiting period the baby is not cared for by his mother it is preferable for him to be cared for in a temporary foster-home rather than in an institutional nursery.

---

[m] The failure of infant tests to predict the future does not of course rob them of their value as an index of present development, a value which may be compared to that of the weight-chart which, irrespective of any predictive value it may have for the infant's future physique, remains a valuable guide to his physical progress during infancy.

To dub a baby unfit for adoption is usually to condemn him to a deprived childhood and an unhappy life. Few are qualified to reach this decision and the grounds on which it is commonly reached today in Western countries are more often well-meaning than well-informed. For instance, many adoption agencies place an absolute bar on the children of incestuous relationships, however good the stock. Naive theories of genetics may also lead to a child being blackballed for such reasons as having a sibling mentally defective or a parent suffering from mental illness. In the days when it was the accepted psychiatric view that all mental illness was hereditary this may have been a reasonable policy. Now that this is no longer so it is unreasonable, except in those cases where the incidence of mental defect or illness in the family is clearly much above the average. It has already been remarked that mental tests have no predictive value in the first 18 months of life, so that some retardation, even in the absence of deprivation, need not be taken seriously unless it is very marked. Finally, the widespread assumption that children with certain physical handicaps are unfit for adoption is ungrounded, as Wolkonir [155] has shown in his interesting paper " The unadoptable baby achieves adoption ".

Three principles thus emerge from discussion of a baby's suitability for adoption :

(a) that an assessment of the child's genetic potentialities requires the opinion of a person with training in human genetics and that in no case should an adverse decision be reached without the opinion of a competent person ;

(b) that psychologists should be thoroughly familiar with the predictive value of their tests and with the effects of deprivation, illness, and other environmental factors on test performance ;

(c) that even if the child's state, or prognoses about his future, are not wholly favourable an attempt should still be made to see whether there may be adoptive parents who, after being given full knowledge of the facts, are prepared in a realistic mood to accept him.

The third area in which knowledge and skill is required is in the appraisal of prospective adoptive parents and in helping those who are suitable to adjust happily to the intense emotional experience of adopting a baby. Here there is no place for the amateur, whose only criteria can be outward signs of respectability, or the worker trained only in physical hygiene with the criteria of income, cleanliness, and cubic feet of air space. These criteria have led to irrelevant and fancy standards. The baby's mental health will depend on the emotional relationships he will have the opportunity to develop ; and their prediction requires good knowledge of the psychology of personality and skill in interview techniques. The principles of the work are admirably discussed by Hutchinson,[80] whose book *In quest of foster parents* should be consulted. She emphasizes the cardinal importance of estimating the real motivation behind the mother's desire to adopt a baby (it being almost always the mother rather than the father who is the architect of the plan). This motivation is often not what it appears to be and its true nature may be largely concealed from the woman herself.

" That foster parents are often searching for love or more love or a different kind of love is not disqualifying, but it is a significant clue to a richer understanding of them. The crux of the matter lies in the degree of normality and reasonableness of their love-specifications. An adoptive mother may insist, in highly rigid and explicit terms, on the qualifications which she wants and must have in a baby. It must be a girl, of specified colouring, age, intelligence, parental status, nationality and temperament. The striking factor is the tenacity with which she may cling to these specifications even after she learns that, practically speaking, her conditions are unreasonable and a hindrance. A prospective adoptive father may be unwilling to deviate from his determination to have a boy who at all costs will fulfil his own frustrated ambition. Such inflexible and narcissistic requests are in contrast to the requests of the foster parent who can easily consider a reasonable range of children and does not come with terms too preconceived or irrevocable."

Those adopting these rigid and inflexible attitudes are doing so for reasons connected with their own emotional conflicts deriving from their own childhoods. In such a case the child is needed not for himself but as the solution of a private difficulty in the parents and, as might be expected, more often than not provides no such solution. The woman who has always felt unloved and who seeks love and companionship from the baby will not wish him to grow up, make friends, and marry. The woman who seeks a little girl who will achieve all that she has failed to achieve is likely sooner or later to be disappointed and to turn against her. Many other unsatisfactory motives may underlie the demand for a child. In the same way satisfactory motives may masquerade under exteriors which seem unpromising. The woman with a gauche brusque manner or the easy-going, untidy, and not too clean couple may none the less have warm hearts and prove loving and effective parents. If their motives are right much else can be overlooked.

How is the social worker to discover their true motives ? Partly by inquiring how it was that they first thought of adopting a baby and partly by learning more about them as people, especially their capacity to make easy and loving relationships with others. In assessing these, three principal opportunities offer—the way they speak about other people, especially their relatives, the way they treat each other, and the way they treat the social worker. The value of these last two criteria are attested in the follow-up conducted by Michaels & Brenner [103] who conclude : " the most fruitful area of exploration in these home studies was the marriage ; the needs it filled for both partners, and the way they achieved their own satisfactions and met each others' needs within it ". Yet, as Hutchinson has pointed out, this is precisely the area most commonly evaded by the interviewer who, unless thoroughly trained, feels, and is, quite incapable of making inquiries which are both useful and yet not embarrassing. Michaels & Brenner proceed :

" The relationship between client and worker also had diagnostic importance. Families who resented the worker's interest in their intimate lives, or felt that their references, position, or deep need for parenthood entitled them to a child with no questions asked, often were reflecting underlying problems bearing an important relation to parental capacity. Often, too, the families who easily established a relationship with a worker, who recognized the agency's need to choose good parents for children and admitted to human qualms, problems, and imperfections, were revealing deep assets for parenthood."

The capacity to face difficulties in a courageous way and to consider soberly how best to meet them is indispensable in adoptive parents for " the ability to take some risks is essential for adoptive parenthood " as it is for natural parenthood.

" The question is not whether we can match their need surely in a child's infancy ; for we plainly cannot. The question is rather what they would do with disappointment ; and whether they could still function as loving parents, satisfied in their parenthood. There is no such thing, unfortunately, as a ' guaranteed adoption ' ; no children an agency can safely mark ' Certified '. It is vital, therefore, that parents be able to accept a child whether or not he can measure up to their hopes and wishes for him " (Hutchinson [80]).

Flexibility and the capacity to face the truth are clearly also desiderata if the parents are to tell the child of his adoption, a practice which all are agreed is essential since sooner or later the truth will become known. Provided the parents can themselves admit the truth and do not have to cling for personal reasons to the fantasy of having produced the child themselves, there need be no great difficulty in bringing the child up from earliest years in the knowledge that he has been adopted. Complications will arise only if the natural and adoptive parents know each other. Reputable agencies usually preserve absolute secrecy on this matter, and there seems no doubt that this is essential if the adoption is not to be jeopardized.

The intense emotional experience of a parent who adopts a baby is often overlooked. Hutchinson has spoken of the " excitement, urgency and deep feeling " which often characterize the adoptive mother's attitude. To her it means not only taking possession for better or for worse of a human life and with it all that the possession of a baby means to a woman, but it may signify also the final acceptance both for her and her husband of the painful fact that they will never have a baby of their own. These are difficult and conflicting emotions which if not worked through adequately may linger to mar the parents' feelings for the baby. Once again insight based on knowledge and skill based on training are required. Similarly, knowledge and skill are necessary in the social worker when she has to tell parents that they are not suitable. Naturally, she will try to put it to them in the most palatable form to avoid distressing them more than necessary, but her principal aim must be to help them see the truth for themselves, for unless this can be achieved the prospective parents will not only feel disgruntled, but will persist in their search for a baby to adopt.

Not much is heard of the black market in babies—the process whereby would-be adopters who have been refused by reputable agencies succeed, sometimes by the payment of large sums to third parties, in securing a baby for themselves. In most countries at present this can be done by people whom all would agree are quite unfit to care for a child. It is a social and legal problem which one day will require attention, but it would be foolish to tackle so thorny a problem before the recognized machinery for adoption is in the hands of qualified people who can be relied upon to make realistic assessments of prospective parents. This will take time.

TABLE XIII. INCIDENCE OF FAVOURABLE ATTI-
TUDES AMONG PARENTS OF ADOPTED
CHILDREN AGED FOUR YEARS PLUS
(MICHAELS & BRENNER)

Attitude of parents	Children	
	number	%
Favourable	26	52
Fairly favourable. . .	18	36
Unfavourable	6	12
Totals	50	100

It has already been remarked that prediction of how a baby will develop is an exceedingly difficult task and for this reason the matching of baby and parents is more easily desired than achieved. Moreover, so long as there are queues of parents waiting for a trickle of babies, the parents may feel thankful to get any child. Race and to some extent colouring can be matched fairly easily, and by matching social class the securing of comparable intelligence is the more likely. Until predictions of other characteristics can be validated, time spent on assessing them is largely window-dressing.

Finally, it may be asked what is the proportion of adoptions which are successful ? This, of course, is a relative question, the results depending largely on the skill of the agency arranging them. What one needs to know is the proportion of successes when adoption is carried out by skilled workers. No such study seems to be available, even that by Michaels & Brenner being concerned with the outcome of adoptions arranged during a period when the agency was changing from a volunteer to a professional basis. The results of this study are given in table XIII.

Regarding the unsuccessful cases, they note " No child ... is poorly housed, clothed or fed, or treated cruelly or irresponsibly by adoptive parents. In this sense none of these homes is bad. The six homes considered unsuccessful are, rather, homes where the child is either rejected, or excessively over-protected and infantilised ". In assessing the meaning of these figures variables such as the age at which the children were adopted and the criteria of success used by the investigators must be taken into account. They must be compared, also, with similar assessments of parents caring for their own children. Judged by the latter standard, so far as it is known, the proportion of successful and unsuccessful adoptions does not seem unsatisfactory. This result is in accordance with clinical experience which does not suggest that an undue proportion of adopted children are referred to child-guidance clinics. From these meagre data it may tentatively be inferred that in skilled hands adoption can give a child nearly as good a chance of a happy home life as that of the child brought up in his own home. Even so, the data are deplorably inadequate and if these problems are to be taken seriously will need to be greatly amplified.

CHAPTER 12

SUBSTITUTE FAMILIES. II : BOARDING-HOMES [n]

It has been insisted throughout this report that the right place for a child is in his own home, or, if he is illegitimate, perhaps in an adoptive home, and because of this measures for preventing family failure (or for arranging permanent and early adoption) have been explored at some length. These must always be utilized to the full before other substitute homes are considered. It is recognized, however, that there are bound to be a few children who will need emergency or more prolonged care outside their homes, and attention must now be turned to the best methods for its provision. First, emergency care will be considered.

Emergency Care

There are many unforeseeable events such as death or sudden illness of the mother which require immediate action for the care of the children. In others, for instance when the mother is going to have a baby or an operation, the need for temporary care is foreseeable. Such cases represent a very high proportion of all those needing care. In England, the Curtis Report [72] quotes them as being about 60% of all children requiring care, while at the Nybodahemmet, through which pass all children over 12 months coming into care in Stockholm, 70% stay from one to eight weeks only (personal communication). Since the circumstances of such children should be well known and the future arrangements either already settled or about to be settled, they are to be sharply distinguished from cases where family discord, delinquency, or neglect pose complex social and psychiatric problems and the future is obscure. The building of large reception homes to which children of all kinds coming into care must go for observation and sorting is not to be recommended, although this is the pattern of the Nyboda in Stockholm and is the pattern recommended by two recent British reports (Blacker [22] and Curtis [72]). The main arguments against such an arrangement are :

(a) that two essentially different problems are confused ;

(b) that there are better alternatives for short-stay children ;

---

[n] This is the term used throughout America and by the League of Nations report to denote private homes which care for children in return for subsistence allowances, but which do not take over legal guardianship. In both these respects they contrast with adoptive homes. In America, the term 'foster-home' is commonly used to cover both types of home, though in England it is usually confined to boarding-homes.

(c) that observation and diagnosis of the potentially long-stay case is usually best done on an outpatient basis (see chapter 13, page 135) ; and

(d) that the size of the institution required to deal with both short-stay cases and observation cases together becomes unwieldy.

There is, however, a place for the small reception centre restricted to taking children over five years of age who unexpectedly require immediate shelter. Their stay should be thought of in terms of a few days only.

There are various alternatives for handling these temporary emergency cases, and different methods need to be employed for different age-groups. For children over six or seven years, especially adolescents, group care in small centres, described in the next chapter, is satisfactory. Children of these ages can fend for themselves for a short time in such an atmosphere and are better not subjected to the strain of having to develop a relationship with the members of an unknown foster-home for a brief time. This consideration, however, does not apply to infants and young children, who all the evidence demonstrates are unable to adapt to group conditions. For them it may be recommended that the plan adopted by several American agencies should become general—the maintenance of a register of foster-mothers who are qualified and willing to take a couple of infants or toddlers for brief periods, and who are paid a retaining fee so that vacancies are always available at short notice. Work of this kind might solve the economic problems of many widows with young children.

It may well be, however, that a better solution for all age-groups lies in mobilizing relatives and neighbours. It has already been remarked that governments and voluntary bodies are slow to support children in their own families and relatively quick to spend money on institutional care. A similar lack of wisdom in spending money is shown when children are taken into care without every effort being made to mobilize relatives to act as substitute parents. It may be that they live far away or that they are not well-off financially. But the cost of railway fares for even some hundreds of miles, together with the payment of maintenance costs, is as nothing to the cost of providing full care for a child. In this connexion, the provision in English law whereby a relative may be officially registered as a foster-mother and paid as such is a most valuable one. Naturally, discretion must be used before mobilizing relatives. If they are complete strangers to the child their value is thereby greatly impaired, while if one of a married couple is opposed to it the child becomes the centre of friction in the new family. Nevertheless, close relatives known to the children are far more likely to have a strong sense of obligation to them than are strangers, and the value of familiarity to the child is boundless.

For the same reasons neighbours may be especially valuable as temporary foster-parents. Not only does the child remain with familiar faces in a familiar place, but the neighbours themselves, because they know the children and their parents, are likely to give the children a warmer welcome and greater security than would strangers. It is thus most important that any child-care agency should do its utmost to foster in each small community a sense of neighbourly pride in the provision of temporary care for its children. Parents should be helped to realize that it is in the children's interests to remain with friends and that it is in their own interests to participate in an arrangement whereby all householders give aid to each other in a family emergency. In fostering such a spirit the agencies themselves must be realistic about standards of physical hygiene. Sometimes it is difficult in a given locality to find houses which meet the usual standards in this respect, but since it is probable that the child himself comes from such a substandard home, no great harm will be done if he spends a few weeks in another such. If, for purposes of temporary care, it were accepted that, provided the foster-home was equal to or better than the child's own home in respect of physical hygiene, no further questions need be asked, many more temporary homes would thereby become available and many more children would be cared for in emergency within sight of their own homes.

Moreover, neighbourhood care of short-stay children would obviate one of the greatest dangers attending the removal of children from their homes—that of the children remaining in temporary care for an indefinite period. To those unfamiliar with the problem this may seem odd, but the reality of the danger is attested by social workers both in America and Europe. Scrutiny of children in institutions and foster-care has on many occasions revealed that a majority of them have lingered on for months and years after the emergency has passed and could have returned home long since. Such inaction appears to spring both from the parents' side and from that of the agency. Some less responsible parents are content to let things slide and, if the case is neglected long enough, come to adapt their way of life to the absence of the children, making conditions increasingly difficult for the children's return. Other parents, of the more simple-minded kind, are impressed by the generous material conditions in which the children are placed and modestly feel they are better off where they are. This attitude, it must be admitted, is sometimes encouraged by agencies, whose pride in the services they render may blind them to the vital need of the child for a continuous intimate relationship which it is so difficult to provide outside his own home circle. This blindness, if coupled with a lack of skilled case-workers, can very easily lead to the agency itself contributing greatly to the very problem it is designed to solve. In the words of an English Children's Officer : [47] " A long-stay case is generally a short-stay case which has been mishandled."

The need for the earliest possible return home of all children placed away is now clearly recognized by all competent agencies, and to enable this to be done it has become axiomatic that a large part of the work of a child-care agency, whether responsible for children in foster-homes or institutions, will lie with their parents.   This is particularly important when the child comes from a home where there is family discord and neglect and where evasions of parental responsibility are too often aided by well-meaning but unskilled methods.

Some Principles of Child Care

In the past, and far too often even now, there has been a reluctance on the part of agencies to recognize the following three principles :

(*a*) A clean cut cannot be made between a child and his home.

(*b*) Neither foster-homes nor institutions can provide children with the security and affection which they need ; for the child they always have a makeshift quality.

(*c*) Day-to-day ad hoc arrangements create insecurity in the child and dissatisfaction in the foster-mother ; realistic long-term plans are essential from the beginning if the child is not to suffer.

An exceedingly common mistake has been the assumption that removing a child from his home will lead him to forget it and to start afresh—and the worse the home, it has been presumed, the more easily will he do so.   This erroneous belief has led to the practice of forbidding parents and children to see each other in the belief that the children will then settle better.   These assumptions flout all that is known about young children and fly in the face of well-attested evidence.   Two studies may be quoted.   In the survey of children evacuated to Cambridge during the second World War, Isaacs and her colleagues [81] found that parents' visits were not detrimental to satisfactory foster-home adjustment and indeed that the reverse seemed to be the case.   Even before this, Cowan & Stout [46] had carried out a systematic study in which they compared the degree of security shown in the behaviour of children who were permitted some contacts with their previous homes (either their own or a foster-home) with that of those who were not. Their results, using the records kept by the social workers responsible for visiting their homes, are presented in table XIV.

It will be observed that the difference in the behaviour of the children according to whether or not they had contact with their previous environment was fairly marked and is in fact statistically significant.   This is the more striking inasmuch as the contact with the previous home was in many cases comparatively tenuous and was not the systematic relationship which would nowadays be recommended.   A particularly interesting subsample consisted of a group of 30 children all of whom had experienced both sorts of change, namely, at least one change where contact with the previous home had been maintained and at least one other where it had not.   The personalities of the children are thus held constant.   The results for this subsample are shown in table XV.

TABLE XIV. COMPARISON OF BEHAVIOUR OF
100 CHILDREN FOLLOWING CHANGES IN HOME
ACCORDING TO WHETHER THEY DID OR DID
NOT HAVE CONTACT WITH PREVIOUS HOME
(COWAN & STOUT)

Type of behaviour	Contact with previous home	
	some	none
	%	%
Insecure	46	67
Secure	54	33
	100	100
Number of changes .	117	430

Note : P is less than .01.

This confirms that the behaviour of the children depends partly on whether or not they maintained contact with their previous environs and is not merely the result of their being different personalities. That this is the case is further demonstrated by case-histories of children whose insecure behaviour had changed to more secure behaviour after contact with the previous home had been permitted.

TABLE XV. COMPARISON OF BEHAVIOUR OF
30 CHILDREN: (a) AFTER CHANGES OF HOME BUT
MAINTAINING SOME CONTACT WITH PREVIOUS
HOME, AND (b) AFTER CHANGES FOLLOWED BY
NO CONTACT (COWAN & STOUT)

Type of behaviour	Contact with previous home	
	some	none
	%	%
Insecure	55	72
Secure	45	28
	100	100
Number of changes .	66	112

Note : P lies between .05 and .02.

These studies confirm what is already known about children—namely that they are not slates from which the past can be rubbed by a duster or sponge, but human beings who carry their previous experiences with them and whose behaviour in the present is profoundly affected by what has gone before. It confirms, too, the deep emotional significance of the parent-child tie which, though it can be greatly distorted, is not to be expunged by mere physical separation. Finally, it confirms the knowledge that it is always easier for a human being to adapt effectively to something of which he has direct experience than to something which is absent and imagined.

It is the realization that the child in a foster-home (or institution) is living in two worlds—the foster-home (or institution) and his own home—which has led to the new outlook on child care. No longer does the social worker imagine that it is possible to find a home which the child will regard as a complete substitute for his own. However good the foster-mother or house-mother, the child will regard her as a more or less poor makeshift for his own mother, to be left as soon as possible. Only if the child is placed before the age of about two is he likely to feel otherwise. And, because the social worker knows how the child will feel, she is able to help the foster-mother to understand the temporary nature of the situation and to adapt to it ; for to encourage a foster-mother to believe that she will get all the satisfactions of a real mother is merely to raise hopes which will be dashed. Moreover, the social worker, realizing the significance which the child's own parents have for him, will realize the necessity, if his future is to be assured, of helping them too. Before, therefore, considering the long-debated issue of how to care for the child away from home, it is necessary to consider some of the essential work which must be done with parents if placement anywhere outside his natural home is to be a constructive step in the child's life and lead to his future happiness, and not to a long-drawn-out period of uncertainty and indecision during which his misery and sense of insecurity lead him either to shut himself in a shell or to become actively troublesome.

Case-work with Parents

Perhaps no child-care practice has been more common or more damaging than that of agencies accepting children from ' bad ' parents on a ' temporary ' basis without plan for the future. This system of indefinite care and uncertain responsibility has been discussed by Gordon [71] on the basis of replies by American agencies to an inquiry.

" This pattern was based on the belief that the parent unable to provide a home could contribute nothing to his child's well-being. Thus agencies felt their duties were discharged when they provided food, shelter and ' training '. Because of this attitude they prolonged temporary placements, discouraged a relationship between parents and their children, ignored the child's need to be deeply loved and to have deeply rooted ties in a family ... The reports show how little case-work help was available to the parents applying for long-term care. One report runs : ' In very few cases have we discussed at the time of placement the specific reason for placement and how long placement should last. In so many cases it would appear that it has seemed " to be the thing to do " to offer foster home placement. The timing has been indefinite '."

Clearly no system is better calculated to discourage the half-hearted parent or to depress a precarious sense of responsibility than to permit an indefinite postponement of decision while relieving the parents of immediate care. This is reminiscent of the hand-to-mouth methods so common in the management of illegitimates.

Instead of unwittingly aiding irresponsibility for the child's future, agencies, whether voluntary or governmental, must make it their first task to help the parents recognize the origins of the problem and make a realistic plan for the future. This means that the agency gives its help conditionally—conditionally on the parents maintaining responsibility for the child's future to the utmost of their capacity. As in all case-work service, the process must begin at the first moment of contact, when the parent's need makes him most ready to face unpalatable truths.

" The parent is held to the need to examine the nature of the neglect, to determine what he can do about it, to explore whether that will help meet the child's needs, and to recognize how the agency stands ready to help him achieve for the child the needed care and security ... [He] must be helped to know the limitations as well as the advantages of boarding care as the case-worker knows them " (Gordon [71]).

Here, perhaps, is the crux of the matter—" as the case-worker knows them ". So long as case-workers do not know these limitations but live, as some do, in the sentimental glamour of saving neglected children from wicked parents, they will act impetuously in relieving parents of their responsibilities and, by their actions, convey to the parents the belief that the child is far better off in the care of others. Only if the case-worker is mature enough and trained enough to respect even bad parents and to balance the less-evident long-term considerations against the manifest and perhaps urgent short-term ones, will she help the parents themselves and do a good turn to the child.

Naturally, by the time parents come to the point of handing over their children, or authorities deem the children to be in need of care, the home situation is likely to be very bad. Immediate and realistic decisions about the long-term future may consequently be impossible. But if the social worker, by her initial handling of the case, makes it apparent that her help is contingent on a long-term solution being found within a reasonable time, and that this can only be one of two alternatives—the parents resuming care for the child at home or releasing him for permanent placement—and that in her view the parents themselves are vital people in the child's life and so must participate in the planning of his future, all but the genuinely psychopathic parents will respond.

Only if the parents are treated in this way, moreover, are they likely to play a useful part in any foster-care arrangements which the agency may make. So long as they are left out of planning, they will either relinquish all responsibility and disappear from the child's life or else interfere in a haphazard and unpredictable way. Such interference is extremely common and constantly complained of ; but it is inevitable when agencies leave the parents out of the planning and leave them also to face alone the complex emotional problems which have so often led to the placement— and the additional problems to which it may give rise, in particular a sense of guilt at having rejected their children and social inferiority at being inadequate parents.

The records of all agencies are full of evidence of the difficulties created for children in long-term care by their parents' inability to permit them to settle in the foster-home and to feel part of it. Parents feel jealous of the foster-parents and make trouble, or they resent them and refuse to visit. The children are left in a turmoil of conflicting loyalties. Pollock & Rose [116] have reported that by far the most difficult cases of disturbed foster-children they were called upon to treat in a child-guidance clinic were those whose parents remained in a conflict of feeling about placement and " carried on an active but irregular connexion with the child ". Of 50 disturbed foster-children attending the clinic in Philadelphia, 17 fell into this category ; they showed a great variety of problems—truancy, stealing, lying, overt sex behaviour, enuresis, speech defects, psychosomatic disorders, severe temper tantrums. In only 4 was successful treatment possible. Pollock & Rose give a full description of the tangled and contradictory motives impelling the parents (the mother in 16 cases and the father in 1) :

" Although the parent voluntarily seeks placement he denies his desire for it from the outset. He sees himself and his child as the helpless victims of unfortunate circumstances created by the death or desertion of the other parent. He protests his love for the child and his interest in obtaining through placement the opportunities for the child which he cannot himself provide. His attitude toward the child may be strongly proprietary, and he is threatened by foster-home placement because he fears the foster-parents may come to ' own ' his child and thereby dispossess him. Or he may project his own need on to the child, identify deeply with it, and try to make the foster-mother serve him, as well as the child, as a good parent. He is critical of the agency's visiting regulations, often complains that they are too restrictive, and then fails to visit as often as it is permitted. He continually assures the child that placement is a temporary arrangement, but always postpones the termination of it. He makes lavish promises and plans extravagant excursions, but they seldom materialize.

" The child, for his part, lives for the visits and gifts from his parent, and has the bitterest kind of rejection or complete indifference towards the placement situation. He refuses to let himself get engaged in any meaningful relationship with foster-parents, and makes it clear that he regards the placement situation as a temporary affair, even though it may go on for years. His attitude toward the placement agency is that it is responsible for his difficulties, since it is, in fact, the agency which has found a place for him to live apart from his parent, with whom he wishes to be. Parent and child form an alliance against the agency, and the latter, in its efforts to aid them in accepting the reality of placement, finds itself carrying a negative, depriving function for both parent and child."

It is evident from this account that the child-care agency had signally failed to deal with the parents' confused feelings—with the most destructive effects on the children. Admittedly such parents are very difficult to manage and it is because of this that case-workers of the highest skill are required at intake, which, as already emphasized, is by far the most hopeful moment for influencing them. And it will be readily observed that the skill required is skill in handling contradictory and unconscious motivation. Only if such skill is available is one of these neurotic parents likely to collaborate effectively with the agency and make the child's placement a fruitful period instead of a pathogenic one. This is a principal reason why child-care agencies are appointing psychiatric consultants to aid them.

Case-work with Foster-Parents

We have emphasized the importance of case-work with parents because, despite its being the key to success and despite its having been strongly advocated in such classics as *Reconstructing behavior in youth*, by Healy et al. (1929), and *Institutions serving children*, by Hopkirk (1944), it is still greatly neglected. Case-work with foster-parents and with foster-children is also vital. Apart from the obvious importance of selecting suitable foster-parents and the need to know both the foster-parents and the child so that they may be sensibly matched, there is the need to prepare foster-parents realistically for the behaviour which the selected child is likely to show. This is too often evaded because of the pressure to find foster-parents and the reluctance to discourage any who may seem appropriate. Yet, unless the case-worker takes the foster-parents into his confidence about the children and their parents, he can hardly be surprised if they are frequently disappointed later and ask for the child's removal—the well-known bugbear of those who arrange foster-home care. They will not behave responsibly towards the agency if the agency fails to behave responsibly towards them. Kline & Overstreet,[87] who have given especial attention to this matter, state that

" it is through the preplacement interviews [numbering usually from two to four] with foster-parents, related to a specific child, that a sufficiently full picture of the personality of the foster-parents is available to enable us to confirm or reject the plan ", and that " the preplacement preparation of foster-parents to receive a child plays an essential role in determining the success of the placement ... Anticipating problems and describing the child's usual patterns of behaviour serve to cushion the reactions of the foster-parents when problems arise. Sharing this information at the outset makes the foster-parents aware that they alone are not responsible for deviant behaviour when it appears and tends to free them from the need to conceal and struggle with the problems alone."

A special part of these preplacement discussions will be concerned with explaining the child's relation to his own parents, the need for them to visit and how they are likely to behave, and the fact that the foster-parents must not expect the child to behave as though he were their own. The nature of the probable long-term plan will be broached, the foster-parents' comments invited, and their participation in planning the future welcomed.

This emphasis on regarding foster-parents as partners in a difficult professional task is comparatively new and is in marked contrast to the traditional relationship in which the child-care worker treats the foster-mother rather as she would a patient. This new professional partnership, moreover, uncovers afresh the running sore of the problem of payments for foster-care. Here the tradition has been to pay a bare subsistence allowance, based usually on the cost of living of some few years previously. There has been much resistance to the idea of a real service fee being paid to the foster-parent and the argument still continues to be used that to do so creates the danger for the child that foster-care may be given for money instead of for love. This hoary argument, which obtains no support from professional social workers, is clung to by governmental agencies for reasons which it is difficult to dissociate from their desire for economy. As Gordon [70] remarks :

"The fear that paying the foster mother will affect the natural affection and concern she has for children is as unrealistic as believing that one's doctor or dentist is less interested in his patient if he may anticipate being paid for his services" (page 216).

Social workers are unanimous that caring for a foster-child is a real job to be paid for, and point out that in days gone by the children used to make their stay economically worth while through work. Moreover, it must be recalled that the letting value of an extra bedroom and the earning possibilities for a housewife through part time work are both profitable alternatives to taking a foster-child. In this refusal to pay foster-parents a proper service fee, coupled with the substantial sums which voluntary and governmental agencies pay for care in institutions, are seen once again the contrasting degrees of generosity with which they support respectively family and institutional care.

In developing the quasi-professional status of foster-parents, it is recommended that they be treated as external members of staff of the agency. It is confidently believed that if this were done, and if they were paid for their services, more responsible foster-parents with better educational background would be forthcoming. Until measures of this kind are taken, national administrations will continue to bemoan the difficulty of finding foster-parents—the universal complaint today.

Case-work with Children in Placement

So far work with parents and foster-parents has been discussed ; but it is time to consider the child, who, as previously remarked, is too often treated as an inanimate object to be posted from one place to another, in the belief that he will not even carry with him the postmarks of the places to which he has previously been sent. The evacuation survey of Isaacs and the follow-up of Cowan & Stout have already been quoted to show that links with previous homes are best maintained and that the idea of ' clean

breaks ' is illusory. Much other evidence shows that the more actively
the child can be helped to participate in the plans being made for him
and the more he is helped to understand what they are, for how long they
will last, and the reasons for them, the more likely is the placement to be a
success. In an attempt to evaluate the quality of service given by the
Maryland Children's Aid Society, Malone [100] followed up 209 children
who had been discharged from foster-home care. Table XVI shows plainly
the increased likelihood of success in foster-care when the child accepts
the placement made for him than when he rejects it.

**TABLE XVI. SUCCESS AND FAILURE OF FOSTER-PLACEMENT ACCORDING
TO ATTITUDES OF PARENTS AND CHILDREN (MALONE)**

Attitude towards placement		Number of children	Number of successes	Success %
child	parents			
accept	accept	147	120	82 } 80
accept	reject	17	12	71 }
reject	accept	31	14	45 } 44
reject	reject	14	6	43 }
Totals		209	152	73

Two points stand out from this table :

(a) the extent to which child and parent adopt the same attitude ;

(b) the importance of the child's attitude, irrespective of the parent's.

The first point is shown by the fact that in 161 of the 209 cases (77%)
the parent and child are in agreement in their attitude and that, of 132
children who accept placement, only 12 (9%) do so against their parents'
wishes. The second point is shown by the proportion of successes being
nearly double when the child accepts the scheme (80%) than when he
rejects it (44%)—a difference which is statistically significant (P is less
than .01).

In her discussion of her findings, Malone remarks particularly on the
difficulty of making successful placements in the case of children removed
from neglectful parents by order of court. In such cases there is usually
no opportunity to prepare the child for placement and it is difficult for
him to understand why he is being removed from home. " He may be
resentful and is certainly not ready nor willing to accept substitute parents."
These facts merit more attention than they have received from those responsible for making court orders.

Because of the great importance of the child's attitude for the success
or failure of his placement, social workers are now giving much time and
attention to discussing with him both the present position and future plans.

This may be done in various ways. One technique is to be particularly recommended—that of the social worker holding joint interviews with parents and child, in which the whole situation is exhaustively reviewed and a common plan reached. Bowlby [28] has advocated this as a method of reducing family tensions and has pointed out that the joint interview, stormy though it often is, is a first-hand demonstration to both parties that the professional worker is neutral and is not arranging things privately with one party behind the other's back, a suspicion which is very likely to arise after individual interviews. Another useful point of procedure is for the child to be given the chance to know something of his new foster-parents *before* placement is made, a technique complementary to foster-parents being given the chance to know something about the child. This information may be conveyed both by verbal description and by personal visits, which may be several in number and include, perhaps, a week-end or two when the child stays with the foster-parents and each gets to know the other. This introductory process is not to be neglected in even young children. Right down to the age of two a phase of mutual introduction is necessary and valuable, for, as is known, nothing alarms a young child more than being left with strangers.

Furthermore, social workers and psychiatrists emphasize how the child needs to be helped in his new relationship if he is not to jeopardize it. In an insightful and clear account of this problem, illustrated by a brief case-history, Baker [6] writes :

" For the child, separation and placement are fraught with emotions of fear, apprehension, anger, despair, and guilt which may be expressed in as many ways as there are defences ... Unless the child can accept the necessity for placement, he cannot use his foster home experience. In his denial of his situation, his energies, either in reality or fantasy, are bent on getting back to his parents."

She describes how the trained case-worker with psychological insight into these complex and conflicting emotions can go far to help the child verbalize these feelings and work through them to an integrated response. Left to himself he may well remain in the confused emotional conflict which results in an incident such as that which she quotes—of the child who proclaimed to the worker on Tuesday that he never wished to see his mother again—his foster-family was his home ; and on Wednesday ran away to his mother !

Not only must the social worker do her best to inform the child of what is going to happen and the reasons for it, but she must not forget that one explanation alone may not suffice nor that the truth which she thinks she has conveyed one day may be overwhelmed the next by misconstructions based either on fantasies or on remarks by parents and foster-parents which have been misleading. The experienced social worker will, therefore, never assume that one explanation is enough—the matter needs to be talked over often, and all the misconceptions dealt with sympathetically. Not infrequently, for instance, children will assume that the home has broken up because of their bad behaviour or that they have been sent away as a punishment—ideas which, if left to embed themselves, can make it impossible for the children to settle in the best of foster-homes and cause great difficulties in later life. In handling these perplexities of children the social worker needs much skill, for children are notoriously chary of confessing their true feelings and adept at camouflage. An apparent desire to go home may cover a fear of returning, and an external equanimity hide a broken heart. Once again psychological skill of a high order is required if the work is to be well done.

The extent to which children grieve over separation from their parents has been little appreciated—indeed it is only in the past decade or so, largely as the result of the work of Klein,[86] that grief in early childhood has been given the central position in psychopathology which it now holds. For long it has been the tradition that the less children were encouraged to express their distress at death or separation the better—they would then get over it more quickly. This view is not supported by modern knowledge. " If the sorrow of death falls upon a family ", writes Spence,[131] " it should not be hidden from the children. They should share in the weeping naturally and completely, and emerge from it enriched but unharmed " (page 38). In helping the children experience their grief, the grown-ups have a vital role to play, whether it is death or absence which is being mourned. As regards absence, Burlingham & Freud,[37] drawing on their residential nursery experience, write :

" Mothers are commonly advised not to visit their children during the first fortnight after separation. It is the common opinion that the pain of separation will then pass more quickly and cause less disturbance. In reality it is the very quickness of the child's break with the mother which contains all the dangers of abnormal consequences. Long drawn-out separation may bring more visible pain but it is less harmful because it gives the child time to accompany the events with his reactions, to work through his own feelings over and over again, to find outward expressions for his state of mind, i.e., to react slowly. Reactions which do not even reach the child's consciousness can do incalculable harm to his normality."

The tears renewed at each visit are always distressing to the grown-ups, who constantly feel that the child is best sheltered from these upsetting events. Only insightful understanding of the part they play in his future emotional development will enable the grown-ups to realize that they are worth while, an understanding made easier by recalling the value to adults of being able to weep over a bereavement.

These emotional responses of children to separation, together with the conflicting feelings which parents often have about relinquishing their children, have led some agencies to place all their new admissions in temporary homes. As Gordon [70] remarks :

" This affords parents and children an opportunity to experience separation and to come to grips with what is involved in this new relationship, by way of preparation for the more extended period of care in a boarding home ... Since the agency can come to know the child and his situation and can help him and his parents to accept the separation with a degree of willingness, the boarding home, to which the child is transferred for more permanent care, is put under less strain and children need fewer replacements " (page 214).

Such a scheme, on the other hand, has the disadvantages of uncertainty, which will be referred to again in discussing observation centres, and it is not easy at present to see where the balance of advantage lies.

The Child of Psychopathic Parents

There is one particular type of child with whom special work is required —the child of parents who are psychopathic and actively bad influences. In handling them the case-worker must first disabuse himself of the notion that because of ' bad heredity ' these children are likely to turn out less favourably than those without such a supposed handicap. Reference has already been made to Theis' follow-up in adult life of children placed away from home [139] and note taken that heredity, so far as it could be determined, had no effect on success or failure : her results may now be given more fully. There were 492 children about whose families something was known. These were divided into three groups according to whether the parents were both fairly satisfactory characters (good), one satisfactory and one unsatisfactory (mixed), or both unsatisfactory (bad). By unsatisfactory is meant parents who were feebleminded, epileptic, alcoholic, immoral, shiftless, etc. The results are given in table XVII.

TABLE XVII. COMPARISON OF SOCIAL ADJUSTMENT IN ADULT LIFE
OF CHILDREN PLACED AWAY FROM HOME,
ACCORDING TO NATURE OF PARENTS' CHARACTERS (THEIS)

Adjustment in adult life	Parentage			Total
	good	mixed	bad	
	%	%	%	%
Socially capable	83	80	71	75
Socially incapable.	17	20	29	25
	100	100	100	100
Number of cases	41	60	391	492

Though the trend is towards those of bad parentage turning out less socially capable in later life, it is only slight and is not statistically significant. (P is greater than .2). It is thus in conformity with the too little known principle of human genetics—that the external characteristics of parents are but a poor guide to the genetic endowment of their children. Healy et al.,[77] though they used a much less reliable criterion of success, had very similar results. They followed up 501 children, 80% of whom were delinquent, to determine how they settled in the foster-homes to which they were sent. They divide them into those with a clear heredity, 105 in number, and those, numbering 396, whose siblings, parents, or grandparents were guilty of crime, gross sex offences, and alcoholism, or suffered from epilepsy, mental deficiency, or mental illness. Their results are presented in table XVIII.

TABLE XVIII. COMPARISON OF SUCCESS OR FAILURE OF FOSTER-HOME PLACEMENT OF CHILDREN ACCORDING TO NATURE OF THEIR HEREDITY (HEALY ET AL.)

Adjustment in foster-home	Heredity	
	clear	adverse
	%	%
Success	74	67
Failure	26	33
	100	100
Number of cases . .	105	817

It will be noted that the 396 children of ' bad heredity ' [o] are represented in the table as 817 cases, which is explained by many of them appearing more than once because of their having ' bad heredity ' in more than one aspect, e.g., alcoholism and crime. The percentages would be little changed, however, if each child were counted only once since percentage success varies hardly at all from aspect to aspect. As regards results, it will be seen that, once again, though the trend is slightly towards the greater failure of those of ' bad heredity ', it is not statistically significant. (P lies between .1 and .2).

In working with children of apparently bad stock results almost as successful as in the case of those from good stock may therefore be confidently expected. This is encouraging. The task, however, remains of discussing with them, or of weaning them away from, parents who are psychopathic and actively bad influences. Once again the tradition has been one of evasion and secrecy and once again it is now known that success demands realism and truth. It might, for instance, be asked, how can the fact that his parents are in gaol, or his mother is a prostitute, be discussed with a child? The problem becomes less difficult if the worker is not afraid of these

---

[o] To dub a child whose sibling, parent, or grandparent is socially unsatisfactory or mentally ill as being of bad heredity is to make an unwarranted assumption, since such data provide no reliable evidence of the genes he carries. For this reason the term ' bad heredity ' is placed within quotation-marks

topics herself and recalls that the child, having lived with such proceedings all his life, may know more about them than she herself does, although he may well be unable to adapt to the manifest conflict between his parents' standards and those he meets elsewhere. Only when the worker can discuss the parents without judgement, spoken or implied, can she help him to consider the problem and understand its implications ; and she needs to realize that one of the principal reasons for his conflict is his determination to see his parents as good figures and his corresponding reluctance to recognize other people's standards as better. This is so important as to warrant a digression.

Throughout this report it has been emphasized that the young child is wholly dependent for his welfare and for life itself on the care bestowed on him by grown-ups, and that, since his parents normally fill this role, it is his parents who are all-important to him. No great war leader saving his country from defeat is more revered than a father or a mother, and it is an inherent characteristic of children to defend their parents' power for good if this is assailed. This was forcibly shown by a group of school-children who were shown a film, designed to teach road safety, in which the father made a traffic error and was corrected by his son, the hero of the story. All the children, despite having identified themselves with the boy-hero who had many feats to his credit, strongly objected to the father of the hero making a dangerous traffic mistake. The father had to be a good and capable father who would not endanger his son's life.

It is this spirit of loyalty and this need to see the parent as good which demand respect and understanding if we are to help a child gradually to grow away from parents who are unmistakably bad influences. If criticizing a parent may lead to a passionate defence and the child's removal to a romantic idealization of the parent, what, it may be asked, is to be our policy ? This has been well described by Jolowicz[84] in her paper "The hidden parent", in which she discusses the secret influence on a child of a parent who, though apparently out of the child's life, is none the less recalled and admired. She gives two case-histories of children from really bad homes who had been with foster-parents from an early age ; though they had appeared to settle down and progress well, both in adolescence had developed all their parents' faults. In neither case, Jolowicz remarks, had anyone dared to talk to them about their parents. Speaking of the girl, whose mother was a prostitute, Jolowicz comments :

" She should have been not only allowed but even encouraged to ask questions, and to speak of her mother. Someone should have acknowledged to her that of course she loved her. Almost everyone loves his mother ; in fact there's something wrong if you do not, not if you do. Once then the child learned that no one would condemn her for wanting to love her mother, and that she no longer had to defend her against the criticisms of people, she could be encouraged to talk of her resentment and anger over the fact that her mother had let her down, had failed to be the kind of mother that she should have been. Through such steps, it would not have been necessary for the child to have repressed her love and hatred to such an extent that they operated like a fifth column within, undermining all the good toward which our efforts were directed. Talking would have released some of the tensions associated with these two feelings and left the child freer to pattern her life after that of the foster-mother's."

This is in fact the experience of those workers who have used this technique with skill. At first the child can admit of no defects in his parent. Then he begins to vacillate between defence and criticism, with outbursts, perhaps, of very bitter feeling. Later again he is able to take a more objective view—to see her as someone with shortcomings as well as virtues, even to understand her as an unhappy person who has made a failure of life. This is often the easier for him if the parent's unsatisfactory behaviour can be related to the difficult childhood she may have had, since the child has first-hand experience of the way in which difficult home situations can create emotional problems for people. By working through violent and contradictory feelings to a more sober and objective view, the child ceases to be the victim of irrational ties to an unsatisfactory parent and is able to make a realistic adjustment to the brutal truth—that his parent is no good to him and that he must seek affection and security elsewhere.

It must be admitted that helping a child in this way is not easy and requires of the social worker not only understanding but emotional toleration of many feelings which are personally upsetting—angry feelings for good parents or foster-parents, admiration for bad ones. Yet, difficult and upsetting though these things may be, they are the forces which will mar the child's life, the time fuses which will lead to explosion if they are not rendered inactive.

This discussion has led time and again to recognition of the need for honesty, for frankness in facing unpalatable truths, and for calling spades spades. Parents need to be encouraged to realize that because of the nature of children's feelings for them they have a tremendous power over their happiness, a power which they cannot abdicate try as they will. Foster-parents are to be helped to recognize the ties which bind children to neglectful parents and to tolerate the cool ingratitude with which the children respond to their beneficence. Children are to be encouraged to express both affection for bad parents and anger for their neglectfulness, emotions which seem either irrational, unnatural, or mutually contradictory. Moreover all three parties, however irresponsible, however ill-educated, however young, are to be encouraged to take part in the planning of the future on a level of equality with the mature, educated, and benevolent social worker. All this may seem topsy-turvy to those still working in the spirit of the nineteenth century, yet these are the great lessons which psychological knowledge has to teach. To Freud is due the credit for discovering not only that human beings nurse in their hearts many fearful and horrifying emotions and are prone to wish outrageous things, but that they have also tremendous capacities for good and, above all, that human nature can master the most distressing facts and the most appalling calamities if it is helped squarely to face the truth.

In discussing foster-placement the emphasis has deliberately been laid on the psychological techniques which should be employed. These techniques of working with parents, with foster-parents, and with the children themselves may seem time-consuming and even fancy, but the issues at stake—the child's future health, happiness, and usefulness as a citizen— and the manifestly unsatisfactory results of more slapdash methods must be remembered. It must be recognized, too, that failure is as often due to lack of skill in planting the child in a new home as it is to the unsuitability of one to the other—the usual reason given. Moreover, it is because the subject has been so neglected that it has been considered essential to discuss the techniques of placement before the methods of selection. To the latter brief attention must now be given.

Matching of Child and Foster-Home

Probably the most important single factor to be borne in mind when selecting temporary foster-homes is that of the motivation of the prospective foster-parents ; this was emphasized also in selecting homes for permanent adoption. Naturally, where temporary placement is the plan and the child is to keep in touch with his own parents, who will be encouraged to visit him, the motives will be different from those found in adoptive parents, but the social worker has to be equally clear about their nature and will find the same techniques of inquiry applicable. Childless couples are not usually very well suited to be temporary foster-parents as they are likely to become too possessive, and success is more common with parents whose children are beginning to grow up. On the other hand, foster-parents over 60 are less likely to be successful than younger ones. But perhaps more important than these criteria is the need for selecting foster-parents who are able to work in close association with a social worker and who are not too proud to ask for and to accept help.

Apart, however, from the question of whether a given foster-home should be used at all is the important matter of matching child and foster-parents. Isaacs and her colleagues,[81] who conducted a survey of over 700 children evacuated to Cambridge during the war, remark that " a great deal of billeting difficulty would have been obviated if the human relationships involved in placement had been given as much thought as the administrative ones ".

In listing a few of the principles to be borne in mind, the conclusions of Isaacs and those which Mulock Houwer drew from his follow-up of 222 children in 152 foster-homes in the Netherlands (personal communication) have been of especial value.

Among favourable conjunctions are :

(a) The presence of other children in the home, especially the siblings of the foster-child. In Cambridge, it was found particularly important for girls over 12 to be placed with other children.

(b) Mulock Houwer found the most successful placements to be where a difference of four years or more (in either direction) existed between the foster-child and the foster-parents' own child of the same sex.

(c) Mulock Houwer also found that the placing of a child of the opposite sex but of the same age as the foster-child worked well.

(d) Finally, Isaacs found that nervous anxious children were best placed in quiet conventional types of home while the active aggressive children were best in free and easy homes with companions, though wherever placed it was this type which gave rise to most difficulty.

Situations to be avoided wherever possible include :

(a) The older the child the less suitable is he for a foster-home. This is especially true of children over 13 years.

(b) Young children (under 10 years) are not well suited to elderly foster-parents (over 45 years).

(c) A foster-child of the same age and sex as a child of the foster-parents gives rise to friction. Such a child is thought of too much for his uses as a playmate and too little for himself. Moreover, situations of jealousy and rivalry are apt more often to arise than where age or sex are different.

(d) Large divergences in standards of living and social class between foster-family and real family have sometimes been found to prove a strain for the child and to make for resentment or jealousy in the real parent. This, however, was not confirmed in the Cambridge survey.

On this matter there are, of course, more-detailed studies available though there does not appear to be a comprehensive review. These limited conclusions are given both as guidance for practice and as an illustration of what can be confirmed or discovered by careful scientific surveys.

The cardinal mistake of placing severely maladjusted children in foster-homes before they are well on the way to recovery has been widely remarked. Some of the first investigators to report it were Healy et al.[77] who analysed the results of placement of 501 cases. " It is striking to find ", they report, " that in 52 per cent of the failures diagnoses had earlier been made of abnormal mentality or personality . . . and 20 per cent more showed personality difficulties ". The same was found in the Cambridge survey of evacuated children : of the 46 cases where placement proved thoroughly unsatisfactory, in 29 (63%) the children had severe emotional disturbances needing treatment. These disturbances were mostly reactions of anxiety and aggression : none was of the shut-in type. Mulock Houwer's findings were similar :

"It appeared that even with the best selection and preparation both of the child and of the parents 20% of the children had difficulties of adjustment in the new family. These difficulties were noted specially with children who in their earliest years had not had contact with their own family or a strong relationship with their mother."

These, of course, are the severely deprived children discussed in Part I.

Binning in Canada (personal communication), on the basis of growth studies using the Wetzel Grid, has emphasized the importance of placing the disturbed child in a suitable institution until growth lag has improved.

The layman has had great difficulty of recent years in accepting the opinions of mental health workers that a very large fraction of children coming into care are emotionally maladjusted. He has complained that psychiatrists and their colleagues see disturbances where none exists and have protested that in any case provided such children are given care and kindness time will heal their troubles. It cannot be too strongly emphasized that those with training in mental health do not share this optimism ; the findings, for instance, of Theis—that 34% of children who had spent five or more years in institutions turned out socially incapable—do nothing to support it. The truth is that in peacetime a child needing prolonged placement is as likely as not to be a maladjusted child and that, unless this maladjustment is recognized and plans for his placement made appropriately, the tragic procession from one foster-home where he fails to settle to another is likely to follow. Foster-mothers cannot for long give loving care to a child who fails utterly to respond. This, as Richman [122] has emphasized, leads to

"a terrific waste in the loss of foster homes ... In the attempt to have the foster home serve all child-placement needs lies, in great measure, the cause for the present break-down of the foster-home program throughout the country [USA]. A serious by-product of this kind of placement is the discouraging effect it has on potential foster-parent applicants ".

Though it is universally agreed that foster-home care is, in general, greatly to be preferred to group care, the unsuitability of certain children for foster-homes makes it necessary to provide group care for them. The following chapter is, therefore, devoted to the principles which should underlie its provision.

CHAPTER 13

GROUP CARE

The controversy over the merits of foster-home care and of institutional care can now be regarded as settled. Though there is no one who advocates the care of children in large groups—indeed all advise most strongly against it, for reasons which will be evident to the reader of the first part of this report—there is widespread agreement regarding the value of small specialized institutions. These have been found to serve best many of the following types of children : [p]

(a) The seriously maladjusted child who is unable until improved to make an effective relation to foster-parents. The organization of treatment centres for such children is discussed in the next chapter.

(b) Adolescents who are no longer dependent on daily personal care and who, partly because they can so easily maintain an emotional relation with their own parents, even in their absence, do not readily accept strangers in a parental role. An exception to this is the adolescent who is leaving school and starting work and who may, as part of the process of earning a living and growing up, settle down easily in a foster-home.

(c) Children over the age of six or seven who are in need of short-term care only.

(d) Children whose parents feel threatened by the relationship between their child and foster-parents and who may need an interval before deciding whether to take their children back home or to release them to live in a foster-family.

(e) Large groups of siblings which might otherwise have to be split up among several foster-homes. (An important exception to this principle of keeping groups of siblings together is in the case of infants and toddlers who cannot in such circumstances obtain the essential individual care they need. This is discussed fully later.)

So many wise books and reports have appeared of recent years on the principles which should be followed in organizing institutions for children (for instance, Hopkirk's [78] in the USA, and the Curtis Report [72] in England) that little discussion is called for here. All are agreed that institutions should be small—certainly not greater than the 100 children suggested by

---

[p] This list has been taken, with slight modification, from Gordon. [70]

the Curtis Report—in order both to avoid the internal regimentation which is inseparable from large establishments and to permit the children to attend the local schools and in other ways to participate in the life of the local community without flooding it. All are agreed, too, on the need for the children to be split up into small ' family ' groups of varying ages and both sexes, each in the charge of a house-mother and preferably also of a house-father, an arrangement which not only encourages some of the emotional atmosphere of a family to develop but also permits of brothers and sisters remaining together to give each other comfort and support. (Nothing is more tragic and destructive of mental health than the system, still all too frequent, which divides children by age and sex and thus splits up families of brothers and sisters.) ' Family ' groups must be kept small ; the Curtis Report recommends 8 as ideal and 12 as the maximum. Informal and individual discipline based on personal relations instead of impersonal rules is possible only in these circumstances. It must be recognized, however, that even in such relatively favourable circumstances it remains very difficult to avoid some of the undesirable characteristics of the institution—uniform regulations between cottages, personal friction between members of staff, and some measure of divorce from the rough and tumble of ordinary social life. Flexibility and allowance for personal idiosyncrasy is apt to be lost and the children have little opportunity for taking part in creating the conditions in which they live. This deadening of initiative and removal of responsibility for creating their living conditions has been too little recognized as an insidious and adverse influence in institutional life.

To overcome it, the scattered cottage-home is widely advocated, an arrangement which can also be described as a large professional foster-home. Thus, local authorities in England are adapting for this purpose pairs of ordinary semi-detached houses on new housing estates and placing a married couple in charge of each. The husband goes out to work, the wife housekeeps, the children mix with the local children and differentiation from the lives of ordinary children is kept at a minimum. For its success this system needs foster-parents of good quality, able to bear considerable responsibility, and these, it must be emphasized, cannot be obtained cheaply. Where foster-parents have not these qualities, and perhaps usually where unmarried foster-mothers are employed, the group of cottage-homes may be better, since it provides more support. Whichever system is adopted certain central services can be provided with attendant saving of labour and cost, though their provision must always be considered against the danger of taking too much personal choice out of the hands of foster-parents. For instance, the central provision of stores removes the need for shopping and the possibility of choice—vitally important parts of domestic life. A compromise between the extremes of central economy with monotony and peripheral variety with increased work needs to be effected.

The responsibilities of house-parents, especially their relations to the children and their parents, are admirably described by Stern & Hopkirk.[136] Among other things, it is emphasized that they must not attempt to own the children and must encourage parents to visit and so promote parent-child relations. That house-mothers require training and that their work should be put on a professional basis is now recognized. It is important, too, that their role in relation to other professional workers—social worker, psychiatrist, and others—should be clarified, so that good team-work is possible. Regular discussions regarding the children in their care should form a recognized part of their duties, and they should be encouraged to discuss their problems with psychiatric consultants, who must of course also be trained for this work.

The medical care of the children must in future include care for their mental health, and in this connexion further experiments are needed in the uses of the Wetzel Grid (for plotting weight and height) as a quick and simple index of emotional well-being. If the findings of Fried & Mayer (see chapter 2, page 29) are confirmed, here is a most valuable tool for detecting emotional disturbance underlying apparent adjustment. These hidden disturbances, often of grave psychiatric significance, are common in institutions. All with mental health training emphasize the deceptiveness of the children's behaviour, especially when it consists of passive conformity. Mulock Houwer, for instance, speaks (personal communication) of the double standard of morals which children in institutions tend to develop : an external conformation with regulations and an internal standard which may be thoroughly delinquent and which only declares itself later. Lawrence in Chicago (personal communication) describes how, when children who had long been in an institution and who there seemed nice and polite were distributed to foster-homes, it was apparent that they were afraid of close personal contacts and seemed to prefer living in an emotional vacuum. They evaded making decisions, resented suggestions of independence, and made excessive material demands. It is important to recognize that these unfavourable traits emerged only when they left the institution —while they were in it all had seemed well, at least to the superficial eye. Similarly Bettelheim & Sylvester [18] have reported on their routine psychiatric examination of a group of six- to eight-year-old children, none of whom was considered in any way abnormal by those who managed the institution in which they lived. Though the first impression of them was rather favourable—" they seemed to have an unusual amount of group spirit "— further examination showed them to lack all adaptability, and both toy-hunger and touch-hunger were prominent. " In spite of psychometrically good intelligence, all conception of coherence of time, space, and person was lacking . . . " Here, in fact, were affectionless psychopathic characters masquerading as normal children ; as might be expected, they had been brought up in the institution from an early age. This leads back to the central theme of this report—the care of infants and young children.

Residential Nurseries

Unfortunately the idea is still prevalent that institutional conditions do not matter in the case of babies and toddlers. It is therefore vital to note that there is no support among those with mental health training for this complacent view. All are strongly opposed to it. Clear statements to this effect are to be found in the writings of all those psychologists and psychiatrists who have undertaken research on the problem. As long ago as 1938 the matter was publicly discussed in the League of Nations report,[90] which tells of the difficulties which institutions experience in caring for " infants and very young children [who] appear to thrive better and to develop more quickly and vigorously under individual attention and in an atmosphere of family affection " (volume 1, page 124). It is therefore distressing to find that eight years later, when much more scientific information was available, the Curtis Committee [72] (which reported to the British Government on the principles to be followed in the care of deprived children) advocated " residential nurseries for all children up to 12 months and for older infants not over $2\frac{1}{2}$ years and not yet boarded out or placed in a family group " (page 160). Clearly this must be regarded as a most serious shortcoming in an otherwise progressive report. It is much to be hoped that this particular recommendation will not be followed either in Britain or elsewhere, and it is satisfactory to find that the official policy of the Children's Bureau of the US Federal Security Agency is against residential nurseries and in favour of the care of infants and young children in foster-homes.

It cannot be too strongly emphasized that with the best will in the world a residential nursery cannot provide a satisfactory emotional environment for infants and young children. This is no mere doctrinaire statement resulting from an excessive preoccupation with the theoretical aspects of the problem : it is the considered opinion of prominent practical workers in many different countries. For instance, in England, Burlingham & Freud reached it as a result of their experience in running a residential nursery during the war. At first they were hopeful of solving the problem, but as time progressed they became increasingly aware of the evil effects of maternal deprivation and of the difficulties of providing substitute care in an institutional setting. Ultimately they concluded (personal communication) that so many helpers were necessary if their infants and young children were to receive the continuous care of a permanent mother-substitute which their observations showed to be essential, that it would be preferable to arrange for each helper to take a couple of children home with her and close the nursery. In the USA Richman [121] came to the same conclusion. After giving details of the nursery and its staff, he ends :

" The number of personnel required to give adequate care to children ranging in age from 9 months to 5 years is greater than for a group of older children ; the expenses of this type of plan, therefore, are very high. The experience with this project supports the evidence reported in child-welfare literature that young children thrive best under individual rather than under group care."

From the Netherlands another practical worker, Mulock Houwer (personal communication), writes strongly criticizing the placement in homes of children under the age of five.

The reasons why the group care of infants and young children must always be unsatisfactory is not only the impossibility of providing mothering of an adequate and continuous kind, but also the great difficulty of giving a number of toddlers the opportunity for active participation in the daily life of the group, which is of the utmost importance for their social and intellectual development. Even in a family with only two or three under-fives and a full-time mother caring for them, it is very exhausting for her to permit the children to ' help ' her in the daily tasks of feeding, washing, dressing, dusting, and so on. When there are many it is almost inevitable for the children to be excluded from these activities and to be expected to be obedient and quiet—namely passive and non-participating. The frustration to which this can give rise is shown by the alternative responses of apathy and violent agression, the extent of which is not easily believed by those without experience of what can go on in such circumstances. This deprivation of the institution child of participation in the daily round of family life and of continuous social intercourse with grown-ups is fully discussed by Isaacs,[82] whose comprehensive account should be read.

Unfortunately national policy in many countries still tolerates residential nurseries, the ill effects of which it is sometimes attempted to mitigate by regulations which, so long as nurseries remain in existence, may perhaps be better than nothing. To avoid the worst effects, the nursery, helpers and children, must be split up into small stable family groups, each preferably with its own pair of rooms—for sleeping, and for eating and playing. Ample toys must be provided with plenty of opportunity for the children to keep some for their very own. A description of these and other techniques for the children's emotional care will be found in the publications of Burlingham & Freud and of Isaacs. Medical inspection, especially against the very prevalent infectious diseases, is now taken for granted, but it is to be hoped that in future this inspection will include also care for mental health. It should become accepted practice that children in nurseries should have psychological tests at regular and frequent intervals, much as they now have their temperatures taken. To make this practicable the present tests might conceivably be abbreviated without losing too much of their reliability, a technical task which it is hoped psychologists will undertake. If such tests were in use, or if the Wetzel Grid were proved to be a reliable index for very young children, at least there would be knowledge of any psychological damage which was being done instead of, as at present, those responsible remaining in ignorance of the matter and able blandly to affirm that the children are ' perfectly all right '. The result of such regular testing may also be expected to hasten the day when residential nurseries, except for the most temporary emergency case, will be commonly recognized as incompatible with sound national policies of mental hygiene.

Study Homes or Observation Centres [q]

All concerned with the care of children away from their own homes have been impressed by the necessity of a thorough knowledge of the child if the right provision is to be made for him. There is much less agreement, however, as to how this knowledge is best obtained.

There are two principle schools of thought : either that there should be residential observation centres, or, on the other hand, that the work is best done on an outpatient basis. The first solution has been accepted in two European countries with national policies for the care of homeless children—Sweden and the United Kingdom. The Child Welfare Board of Stockholm has laid it down that all children needing foster-care must pass through their large centre, built in 1938, which also houses short-stay children. Observation and diagnosis are carried out during a stay of some weeks or months with the assistance of a full-time child psychiatrist and a number of kindergarten teachers trained in play techniques. In the last two years the United Kingdom has also officially adopted this policy, partly as a result of Swedish experience. The Curtis Report [72] has an important paragraph on the subject :

" We do not consider that children who come into the charge of the authority above the nursery age should be immediately placed in the Home in which they are to remain. We have received almost unanimous recommendations from our witnesses in favour of what are variously described as reception homes, sorting homes, or clearing stations. The need for these is, according to witnesses from the Ministry of Health, one of the important lessons learnt from evacuation experience " (page 161).

Following this report and the Children's Act which resulted from it, a memorandum has been issued by the British Home Office [73] stating, in regard to children over two years of age likely to need care for more than six months :

" in order to obtain the fullest possible knowledge and understanding of a child's health, personality, conduct, intellectual capacity, emotional state and social history, provision must be made for his reception and temporary accommodation in a place where facilities are available for enquiry into these matters and for observation by a skilled staff."

There are many workers with mental health training in both Sweden and the United Kingdom who believe that a policy whereby *all* such children

---

[q] These terms are used here to denote centres which have as their purpose the observation and diagnosis of children. The term ' reception centre ' is also used for this purpose, e.g., by the British Home Office,[73] but is not used in this sense here to avoid confusion with centres having the very different function of providing emergency shelter to which it is also applied (see p. 110).

have to pass through an observation centre is greatly mistaken, and this view is sustained by many with experience of the matter in the USA. Those who take this opposite view believe, first, that it is better for the child not to be subjected to an inevitably unsettling experience and, secondly, that diagnosis can be made as well or better by outpatient methods. They believe that the Curtis Committee and its witnesses, though right in stressing the need for accurate diagnosis, were wrong in jumping to the conclusion that this could be arrived at only under residential conditions. In particular, they believe that the lessons of wartime evacuation experience, when large numbers were being dealt with in a large-scale emergency, were misleading when applied to peacetime conditions.

The first question must be : can accurate diagnoses be made under outpatient conditions ? If they can, the expense and effort of setting up observation centres is clearly unjustified—and many child psychiatrists and social workers with experience believe that they can. Clothier,[44] a child psychiatrist with extensive experience of the problem in Boston, writes : " Ordinarily study cases are best studied in outpatient clinics against the background of their own homes." Richman,[122] a child case-worker in Cleveland, after remarking on the artificiality of separating study from treatment and the unsettling effect of study homes, comes to the same conclusion. Finally, Wildy & Gerard report (personal communication) that the agency of which they are director and consultant psychiatrist respectively, the Illinois Children's Home and Aid Society, closed its observation centre as a result of experience. They had found that the most relevant diagnostic information was contained in the social history taken by a skilled social worker, to which could be added a psychological and physical examination carried out in an outpatient clinic. Information, obtained at first hand by the social worker, on the child's behaviour in his home and on his relation to herself during a brief outing made for the purpose, they believe, is more reliable for prognostic purposes than that obtained in the conditions of a reception centre.

One of the difficulties in reaching a diagnosis is, of course, that of deciding whether difficult behaviour or neurotic symptoms are reactions to present adverse circumstances or are already embedded in the child's personality. In tackling this problem it is possible, in addition to clinical examination, to proceed along two different lines—(a) that of taking a detailed history of the child's behaviour and symptoms in all known situations, present and past (at home, in school, with relatives, with foster-parents, etc.), and of his personal experiences in relation to grown-ups, especially parents, and (b) that of removing him from his home and placing him in an entirely new environment. Those with experience regard the former line as the more reliable since it taps a much wider variety of information. Moreover, the second method is deceptively simple and can be very seriously misleading, since it is notorious that children are apt to behave in an uncharacteristic way in strange surroundings. This is particularly true of children under five, as every nursery-school teacher knows and as Murphy [108] demonstrated in her well-known study. Overt behaviour in this age-group, she showed, depends on factors such as space, personality of grown-up, and the number, age, and sex of other children : " a child may be extremely sympathetic one day in one group and very aggressive the next day with a different combination of children ". Moreover, children are bound to be affected by the situation in which they find themselves at the time, or more precisely which they *believe* they are in at the time, which may be very different and very difficult to discover. In this connexion, Wollen,[156] a psychiatric social worker with experience in a pioneer observation centre in England, has remarked :

" In some cases their behaviour is controlled by fear of the possible consequences of misbehaviour repercussing unfavourably on their future. They are also anxious to be accepted by the adults, purchasing favour and, as they hope, security. It is impossible to convince the children that by being good they will not be able to remain indefinitely at the Centre. In others, personal anxieties temporarily distort their behaviour. The neurotic and maladjusted child, who can be diagnosed in a psychiatric interview, is not always obviously disturbed in his behaviour in the Centre."

So far from recognizing the elementary error of supposing that a child's behaviour in what is apt to be described as a ' neutral and friendly atmosphere ' is characteristic of him, the inexperienced observer is apt to cling with extraordinary tenacity to the view that what he happened to see of the child is of tremendous significance. Tommy was seen to hit another child three times—therefore he is an aggressive boy. Mary spent hours sitting by herself in a corner—therefore she is a solitary child. Such conclusions may, of course, be true, but it is known they are sufficiently often false to call into question the whole value of observations made in these artificial surroundings.

Wollen also points to the danger that a stay in a reception or observation centre may come to be regarded by administrators as a quick and easy solution of family difficulties and that children will consequently be unnecessarily removed from their homes. As such it may become a bad substitute for thorough social investigation and family case-work. This is, no doubt, a grave danger. Indeed, it is probably only because of the lack of adequate social and child-guidance services that the belief in the necessity for widespread observation centres has developed.

Further, the danger that a stay in an observation centre will have an adverse effect on the child and his parents must be noted. Psychiatrists in Stockholm have been concerned to find that some children passing through the city's observation centre show signs of ' hospitalism ' on reaching their foster-homes (personal communication). The pioneer centre in Kent, England,[102] reports that " removing a child from its home, even for a short period of investigation, can have an adverse effect upon his relationship with his parents, especially when the removal comes after a family crisis which may have made him feel hostile to them or rejected by them ". Children under five or six, of course, are particularly vulnerable to these experiences. The report rightly emphasizes that " any effective attempt to reassure the child must be based on an understanding of his private terrors and regrets, which he may hardly have recognized clearly himself ". It underlines the need for " as early and close a contact as possible between the child and the social worker or official who will be dealing with him after he leaves the Centre ". In all this, needless to say, absolute frankness with the child regarding his position and his future is essential. With all these provisos, however, it is exceedingly difficult to make the stay a therapeutic and constructive one and not just one more period of unsettlement and anxiety. Neither should the adverse effect on parents be forgotten—family ties and the sense of responsibility are not encouraged by the children's removal.

Though the conclusion may be drawn that for the great majority of children observation centres are unnecessary and for children under five a danger, there will always be a small minority for whom temporary care for investigation is needed. These are particularly children who have no home whatever or about whom it is impossible to obtain a reasonably adequate history, conditions which are apt to coincide. In the USA, the practice has grown up of placing these children in temporary foster-homes specially selected for the purpose. In such conditions there is greater opportunity to reach a sound appraisal of the child's capacity to make relationships with parent-substitutes and, therefore, to assess his potential development. Some foster-parents, especially those who have had children of their own, are interested in this special work, for which they must, of course, be properly paid.

Children who are clearly very disturbed emotionally are best placed at once in a treatment centre for child psychiatric cases, more of which are needed in all countries. Children deemed by the courts to be in need of care and protection are usually best observed while remaining at home. Another week or two in unsatisfactory conditions is unlikely to make a difference to their future, and a smooth and planned transfer to other conditions will make for successful placement. The impetuosity and impatience of the outraged official must be resisted.

It is probably only for the older boy or girl who is a delinquent and a danger both to himself and to others that observation centres are really needed ; these are usually called remand homes and their consideration lies outside the scope of this report.

* *
*

To sum up, then, it may be said that group residential care is always to be avoided for those under about 6 years, that it is suitable for short-stay children between 6 and 12, and for both short-stay and some long-stay adolescents. It is also indispensable for many maladjusted children, with whose care the next chapter deals.

———

CHAPTER 14

CARE OF MALADJUSTED AND SICK CHILDREN

Care of Maladjusted Children

There are three groups of children away from their homes who need special psychiatric care :

(*a*) Those who are suffering from psychiatric disability and who are removed from their homes by legal, medical, or social agents for reasons either of therapy or social restraint. Such disabilities may or may not be the result of bad home conditions.

(*b*) Those, such as were described in the last chapter, whose psychiatric disabilities have been caused by their experiences in institutions and foster-homes.

(*c*) Those whose disabilities have resulted from the adverse experiences in their own homes which were the cause of their coming into care—for instance, cruelty, broken homes, and emotional neglect.

The first group, it will be seen, is to some extent the obverse of the third, depending on whether it is the maladjustment of the child or the unsuitability of the home which is chiefly emphasized.

It has already been remarked that in the early years of the child-guidance movement workers were apt to remove children from their homes too lightly, that in some quarters the whole movement had come into bad odour for this fault, but that methods were now changing. Many leading workers today regard the removal of the child as a last resort and a confession of failure, for what removal by itself can never do is to solve the underlying emotional conflict. Too often the results of such a policy are to hide the real problem and to create new ones. Moreover, only two outcomes are possible ; either long-term care has to be provided, which is known to be both difficult and expensive, or else the child has sooner or later to be returned to the same conditions from which he came. These long-term considerations are too often ignored in face of the temptation to use a relatively easy short cut. Only if the social worker, the doctor, or the magistrate has a well-considered long-term plan for the child is it permissible to remove him from his home for his own good. Without such a plan his removal is merely the creation of yet another deprived child.

But even if great caution is exercised in removing children from their homes and even if far better measures are introduced to prevent

children becoming maladjusted, there will be a need for many years to
come to care for many maladjusted children away from their homes.
Though many with less overt difficulties and even some delinquents may
be handled in foster-homes (Kline & Overstreet [87] give an interesting
case-history of a disturbed 15-year-old girl helped in this way), it is widely
agreed that the majority of the more aggressive and delinquent characters
must first be helped to a better social adjustment. How is this to be done
and in what conditions ?

Clothier,[44] in a useful paper, has reviewed the variety of residential
accommodation necessary if all children—those of different ages and
with different disturbances—are to be catered for. This report will do no
more than formulate certain general principles to be followed when dealing
with children aged six years and over.

First, all the specifications described for institutions in general apply.
Children must be split into small groups which are best housed in separate
cottages or flats, with their own house-mother or father. Sometimes these
will be grouped together as a ' village ', as for instance at Skå in Sweden
or at the Hawthorne-Cedar Knolls School outside New York ; or as in
Chicago where an urban experiment is being made by the Jewish Children's
Bureau and a small building containing three flats has been erected so that
it merges into its surroundings, each flat being in the charge of house-
parents who care for six children. An alternative arrangement is for cottages
to be scattered over a limited area, as in the case of the war-time hostels
in Oxfordshire described by Winnicott & Britton.[150, 151] Each plan has its
advantages, the main one of the scattered arrangement being that each
hostel or cottage can develop its own private way of living according to
the personalities of the house-parents and without awkward comparisons
being made by the children.

In regard to the mixing of sexes and ages, there is considerable diversity
of practice, in the case of maladjusted children the trend being towards
separating pre-adolescents from adolescents, and separating the sexes also
once adolescence is reached. Not all would accept the desirability of these
divisions however. But there is no divergence regarding size of group :
all agree it must be kept small. Winnicott & Britton [150] state that 12 children
seems the ideal number ; though at Skå the number is 7 and at Hawthorne-
Cedar Knolls, where many of the children are adolescent, as many as 16.
Clothier,[44] in discussing arrangements for pre-adolescents, has proposed
6 to 10. These variations are probably not as contradictory as they may at
first sight appear and are dependent largely on the age of the children for
whom provision is being made. The younger the fewer is a sound principle.
It will be seen in any case that none of those professionally concerned
recommends more than about 16 children in a cottage, even in the case of
adolescents, and the maximum of 25 suggested by the British Ministry
of Health,[75] on the basis of experience with wartime hostels for difficult

children, cannot be endorsed. Such a number may be compatible with tolerable custodial care, but is too many if therapy is to be attempted, unless, of course, broken up into subgroups, each with its own house-parents.

Nomenclature, it will be observed, varies—foster-home, hostel, treatment unit, school, are all in use. Probably treatment unit is the most satisfactory, provided that treatment really is provided. It highlights the real problem, namely that the child is psychiatrically ill and requires treatment, and has also been found (by the Jewish Children's Bureau of Chicago, personal communication) to be more acceptable to parents than other terms, because it makes it clear that something more is provided than could be expected of the parents themselves. The terms ' foster-home ' or ' hostel ' lack this implication.

As in the case of normal children, it is imperative that maladjusted children should be kept in touch with their parents, both by receiving visits from them and by making holiday visits to their home. Moreover, there is the same need for case-work with parents—a need too-easily neglected. Robinson [124] of Wilkes-Barre, Pennsylvania, USA, has emphasized this need and also the need for a properly considered long-term plan, in the making of which the child and his parents should participate. As regards parents' difficulties, he writes :

" The child's progress, especially as it is reflected in behaviour, will often uniquely arouse the feelings of parents. It is challenging to see a child realize accomplishment which he could not reach at home and the parent may respond in a variety of ways. He may, for example, feel more intensely the separation which he has arranged between himself and his child and want to re-establish the closeness out of which so much of their difficulty had grown. He may feel antagonistic to the treatment center and attempt to project on the center the responsibility for his child's being away from him. He may be unable or unwilling to recognize changes in the child. His feelings of rejection may come frankly to the fore. He may at once experience a new measure of common feeling with his child. Whatever the parent's response, it brings into relief the quality of parental nurture which has complemented the child's development. Work with the parent needs to be closely related to what he encounters in the child's newly emerging self and the manner in which he can more satisfactorily fulfil his parental rôle."

Because of the necessity of closely integrated work with parent and child, treatment centres should confine themselves to taking children from within a reasonable distance of the centre, a consideration which demands that such centres be scattered widely throughout a community.

All are agreed that the success or failure of the centre will turn on the personalities of the house-parents, on the selection of whom Winnicott & Britton [150] have many wise things to say :

" We find that the nature of previous training and experience matters little compared with the ability to assimilate experience, and to deal in a genuine, spontaneous way with the events and relationships of life. This is of the utmost importance, for only those who are confident enough to be themselves, and to act in a natural way, can act consistently day in and day out. Furthermore, wardens are put to such a severe test by the children coming into hostels that only those who are able to be themselves can stand the strain."

Though Winnicott & Britton, and also the British Ministry of Health,[75] have been inclined to regard previous training and experience as of secondary importance, this is probably because hitherto there has been no training which has had much relevance to the work to be done. Once it is recognized that the task is one of making skilled human relationships with children who have had their capacity to do this greatly impaired, the need to train house-parents, practically as well as theoretically, in the psychology of human relations and of child development is discerned. This work must certainly be professionalized—just as nursing has become professionalized—and all workers must become proficient in the principles and practice of mental health. Only with such training is it possible to expect them to tolerate the triad of symptoms which all must understand—aggression, depression, and regression—and to acquire skill in handling them. And not only must the house-parents understand these things, they must also be able to teach their domestic staff about them, since in a small unit all must follow similar principles and the relations of the children to the domestic staff are of the greatest importance.

The children's need to test the hostel staff to see if they really are good and really can tolerate and manage their aggressiveness and greed has been discussed fully by Winnicott & Britton : [150]

"Each child, according to the degree of his distrust, and according to the degree of his hopelessness about the loss of his own home (and sometimes his recognition of the inadequacies of that home while it lasted), is all the time testing the hostel staff as he would test his own parents. Sometimes he does this directly, but most of the time he is content to let another child do the testing for him. An important thing about this testing is that it is not something that can be achieved and done with. Always somebody has to be a nuisance. Often one of the staff will say : 'We'd be all right if it weren't for Tommy . . .', but in point of fact the others can only afford to be 'all right' because Tommy is being a nuisance, and is proving to them that the home can stand up to Tommy's testing, and could therefore presumably stand up to their own."

Because of this type of behaviour and because of the intensely personal relationships necessary, it is widely recognized that house-parents must be given the choice of accepting or refusing a child. A warm personal relationship with tolerance of much difficult behaviour cannot be provided to order. Moreover, each pair of house-parents will find one sort of difficulty easier to handle than another. For these reasons the policy of organizing groups of hostels, permitting each to be a little different, such as those described by Winnicott & Britton, has much to recommend it.

Much has been written on methods of discipline in treatment centres of this kind, and the literature has been usefully reviewed by Brosse.[31] All are agreed that methods must be informal and relatively free and based essentially on close personal relationships between grown-ups and children instead of on impersonal rules and punishments. Democratic regimes in which the children themselves play a major part in the control of the community are often practised with advantage, but they must not be thought of as sufficient in themselves, while several limitations in their use need to be observed. First, the growth of self-government cannot be forced and must be built step by step with the help of adults skilled in community work. Secondly, children under 11 cannot manage self-government, except in minor matters, and should not be exposed to the strain and chaos which is likely to ensue if it is tried. Vulliamy [144] believes that it is only when the group contains a number of children over 14 years that anything extensive can be made to work. Thirdly, as Winnicott & Britton [151] have remarked, children who have been deprived of a satisfactory early home experience have not the inner resources necessary to enable them to participate in self-government. Self-government is thus no panacea, though appropriately introduced it can be of great value.

As regards education, it is desirable, whenever possible, for children to go to the ordinary local schools, but it must be recognized that many of them are too ill psychiatrically either to benefit from or to fit into such schooling. In these cases tuition must be provided on the premises, which is, of course, more easily done if the centres or cottages are grouped as a ' village ' than if they are scattered.

In this as in other matters a good deal of flexibility is necessary and rigid administrative machinery which divides schools from hostels is to be deprecated.

Treatment

So much for the general background for the caring of maladjusted children over the age of six or seven years in groups. What of treatment ? It has three aspects :

(*a*) the utilization of the total social group for therapeutic ends ;

(*b*) the development of a therapeutic relationship with a staff member ;

(*c*) the provision of individual psychotherapy or counselling.

Different workers in this new and developing field hold rather divergent views on the relative balance of these three therapeutic forces, though all would agree that each has its place. Much has been written as regards the first by those concerned in the development of self-governing communities, which are of especial value for adolescents who are not too disturbed. A different aspect of the value of the group is the way in which children act as alter egos for each other, a process which has been noted by Winnicott & Britton and also by Bettelheim & Sylvester, who give a case-history illustrating it. Bettelheim & Sylvester [17] also demonstrate the way in which other children can by their behaviour to a newcomer help him to get insight both into his behaviour and into his fantasies. They emphasize especially how " the emotionally disturbed child frequently mistrusts verbal statements. It is the actuality of the child's experiences within the group which achieves therapeutic results."

Probably all would agree that, therapeutic though relations with other children can be, it is the relations with grown-ups which carry the main therapeutic load. In utilizing these there is some divergence of practice, some workers advocating an identity between house-parent and therapist and others, probably a majority, preferring the roles to be filled by different workers. The advantages and disadvantages are partly technical and partly those of expediency and it would be out of place to argue them here, though there is some ground for thinking that more adequate attention is given to the parents' problems and the parent-child relationship by workers who separate the roles than by those who fuse them. When roles are separated the therapist is usually the social worker who has handled the case from its inception and who has therefore made relations with both child and parents. She may well have entered into a therapeutic relationship with the child before he has left home and may continue treatment after he has returned, a plan which a house-parent is unlikely to be free to follow. By so doing she acts as a continuity figure of great importance.

In all countries there is much debate in medical circles regarding the therapeutic role of non-medical workers, but, though they still have their critics, it is safe to say they have come to stay. Those psychiatrists who have actually had experience of working with social workers and psychologists in this way are almost unanimous regarding their value, though they would emphasize the need for them to be properly trained and to work in close collaboration with an experienced medical psychotherapist. It is interesting to note that one of the great pioneers of psychologically-based residential work with deprived children, the Austrian psycho-analyst Aichhorn,[2, 3] was himself non-medical. His book, *Wayward youth*, has been an inspiration in many countries.

The relation of the child to therapist and house-mother can run the whole gamut of maladjusted behaviour—remoteness and refusal of contact, hostility, clinging babyishness, and every combination of them. Of the three, remoteness is the most pathological, clinging babyishness the most hopeful, for the basic need which has been repressed as a result of frustration is the intense oral dependence on the mother and the need to have her always there—in short the need for mothering. Once the child has been able to trust a mother-figure sufficiently to permit himself to express this need and to regress to an infantile relationship, a major step has been taken, though to the uninformed his behaviour may seem deplorable. The rationale for this treatment has been well described by Winnicott & Britton : [151]

" In the majority of cases children who were difficult to billet had no satisfactory home of their own, or had experienced the break-up of home, or, just before evacuation, had to bear the burden of a home in danger of breaking up. What they needed, therefore, was not so much substitutes for their own homes as *primary home experiences* of a satisfactory kind.

" By a primary home experience is meant experience of an environment adapted to the special needs of the infant and the little child, without which the foundations of mental health cannot be laid down. Without someone specifically orientated to his needs the infant cannot find a working relation to external reality. Without someone to give satisfactory instinctual gratifications the infant cannot find his body, nor can he develop an integrated personality. Without one person to love and to hate he cannot come to know that it is the same person that he loves and hates, and so cannot find his sense of guilt, and his desire to repair and restore. Without a limited human and physical environment that he can know he cannot find out the extent to which his aggressive ideas actually fail to destroy, and so cannot sort out the difference between fantasy and fact. Without a father and mother who are together, and who take joint responsibility for him, he cannot find and express his urge to separate them, nor experience relief at failing to do so. The emotional development of the first years is complex and cannot be skipped over, and every infant absolutely needs a certain degree of favourable environment if he is to negotiate the essential first stages of this development."

In addition to the work of Winnicott & Britton in England, now unfortunately brought to an end, treatment based on these conceptions is proceeding in Sweden and the USA. Reference has already been made to that by Jonsson at Skå, where children are given opportunities for highly regressive behaviour including taking all their food from a baby's feeding bottle. The same permissive atmosphere is described by Bettelheim & Sylvester with the same hopeful results. In one of their papers [18] they give in some detail the case-histories of two children grossly deprived in early childhood who regressed to babyish ways before getting better. One boy of ten, who had been brought up in various institutions and had attempted suicide, began after some weeks to behave like a small child to his house-mother who was also his therapist (or counsellor).

" In baby talk he called her his mother, saying, ' My mamma washes my hands for me. She gets me clean socks '. He asked her to help him dress and to spoon-feed him. He was permitted to experience this primitive child-adult relationship. Two months later, baby talk and desire for spoon-feeding were given up spontaneously and new aspects appeared in his relationship with his favorite counselor."

Later, however, he regressed temporarily once more and this time discovered a baby's bottle and fed himself from it. This process of reverting to infantile ways in order to restart the growth of primary relationships from a new and better basis takes time, so that stays in treatment centres are matters of years not months. This impresses once again the over-riding necessity of preventing these conditions developing.

Finally, the great problem of dealing with severely maladjusted children between the ages of three and six who cannot remain at home must be noted. Group care is clearly unsuitable and the provision of clusters of small homes where skilled professional foster-mothers can care for them in tiny families of one or two while they receive treatment is probably the answer. This is inevitably expensive, but the returns for money expended on therapy in these early years are so infinitely greater than at any other age that it would almost certainly prove the wisest of investments.

Developmental work in this field is called for. It is to be hoped that it will appeal to institutions and foundations in a position to sponsor it.

Care of Sick Children

It will be evident that all the principles for the prevention of deprivation in children apply equally to the physically sick as to the physically fit, yet this has been all too little recognized by the medical profession and bad cases of deprivation are still to be found in children's hospitals. It is true that leading paediatricians in many countries—among them Debré in France, Wallgren in Sweden, Bakwin and, until he died, Aldrich in the USA, Spence and Moncrieff in Britain—are alive to the problem, but there remains a great lag in reform. More serious, some paediatricians are still unaware of the importance of the matter, though their number is dwindling.

Spence,[132] in his lecture on "The care of children in hospital", has given a vivid picture of deprivation in children's wards, fully as bad as that to be found in the worst of the large institutions now universally condemned. He refers especially to the isolation, aimlessness, and uncertainty of children in long-stay hospitals. Referring to his service on the Curtis Committee, he says :

"I have had to listen to a great deal of evidence from men and women who spent much of their childhood and adolescence in these institutions. The sensitive and intelligent witnesses recalled with nightmare memories the long hours of winter evenings which pressed upon them in their adolescence, the aimlessness of their existence, the uncertainty of their future. They had their lessons each day, and raffia work and entertainments, but there was no intimacy with anyone who could explain to them the purport of their illness or encourage them with plans for the future. The fault lies in the form and arrangement of most of these long-stay hospitals. They have been conceived too much as medical institutions and arranged too much as hospital wards."

What are the solutions ? As usual, the first must be to keep the children at home whenever possible. In this connexion Spence writes :

"I have experimented in the domestic care and treatment of children with active abdominal tuberculosis, of children immobilized by orthopaedic appliances, of children with chronic disease which requires frequent observation and examination ; and from these experiments I am convinced that too often and too lightly is the decision made to confine children in long-stay hospitals."

Medical officers in the English county of Middlesex have for some years advocated treating young tuberculous children in their homes and believe better results are obtained than by sending them to sanatoria. In this connexion the remarkable development of home care for chronically ill patients by the Montefiore Hospital [104] in New York City may well be relevant. This hospital has set out to treat as many patients in their own homes as in its wards, and has organized for this purpose a major department with its own medical and nursing staff, social workers, equipment to send out on loan, motor transport, and a housekeeper service. The medical director, Bluestone, claims that this has been an unequivocal success, with especial " value to the patient and his family derived from the patient's ability to participate in normal family living despite the limitations imposed by his illness " (page 17). Costs per head per day of care are no more than 25% of what they are in hospital. Although comparatively few children have been treated, since it is not primarily a children's hospital, the same principles apply. Indeed, the very fact that almost all children have an adult to care for them at home means that the housekeeper service, which is an indispensable part of the home medical care of many adults, especially women, is less necessary. This pioneer work of the Montefiore Hospital may well lead to a great revolution in hospital practice and one which, from the point of view of the prevention of children being deprived, would be of the utmost value.

In those cases where children must come into hospital much can be done to minimize the emotional shock. In the case of children under three, Spence [132] has long advocated whenever possible the admission of the mother with her baby.

" I have worked under this arrangement [in the hospitals at Newcastle-upon-Tyne] for many years, and I count it an indispensable part of nursing in a children's unit. Nor is it a revolutionary idea. By far the greater part of sick children's nursing is already done by mothers in their homes. Not all illnesses will be suited to this nursing, but the majority of all children under the age of 3 derive benefit from it. The mother lives in the same room with her child. She needs little or no off-duty time, because the sleep requirements of a mother fall near to zero when her own child is acutely ill. She feeds the child ; she tends the child ; she keeps it in its most comfortable posture, whether on its pillow or on her knee. The sister and nurse are at hand to help and to administer technical treatment to the child. The advantages of the system are fourfold. It is an advantage to the child. It is an advantage to the mother, for to have undergone this experience and to have felt that she has been responsible for her own child's recovery establishes a relationship with her child and confidence in herself which bodes well for the future. It is an advantage to the nurses, who learn much by contact with the best of these women, not only about the handling of a child but about life itself. It is an advantage to the other children in the ward, for whose care more nursing time is liberated."

In New Zealand, in 1942, Pickerill & Pickerill [113] built a plastic-surgery unit for babies and toddlers especially planned with bed-sitting-rooms in which the mothers could nurse their children themselves. Though this was done principally to prevent cross-infection, in which it has been wholly successful, Pickerill & Pickerill are also greatly impressed by its value for both mothers and babies.

" These babies want mothering more than expert nursing. With their mothers they are happier, more contented, and are able to have more constant attention day and night, and an operation for a contented baby is much more likely to be successful . . . The mother is just as proud of the result as we are."

This arrangement is increasingly approved by paediatricians and it is to be hoped that new hospitals for babies and young children will all be built on this principle. Fortunately, many of the less-developed countries have never forsaken this natural arrangement.

A complementary service which should, of course, be available when required is a housekeeper service to care for other children who may be left at home.

Older children who must be admitted to hospital can be prepared for their stay and accompanied to the hospital by their mothers, who will undress them, put them to bed, and see them off to sleep. Nothing is worse than telling the child a fairy tale, perhaps about a party, followed by the sudden disappearance of the mother leaving the child aghast, either silent or screaming, in the hands of a stranger. Regular visiting by the parents is to be encouraged (fortunately it has been found not to increase cross-infection[146]), since it not only increases the child's happiness and sense of security while in hospital but reduces emotional disturbances after his return. Children between the ages of three and six need frequent visiting, daily if possible ; older children can manage longer intervals. Regular formal visiting-hours, it has been found, are a mistake. Instead it is better to encourage mothers to drop in frequently and casually, perhaps when they are out shopping, and stay for relatively brief periods during which they should be allowed to feed and bath their children and to give them small presents. An interesting account of some of the difficulties of arranging visiting in a children's ward and of how they can be overcome in the case of children over three has been given by Sharp.[129]

Though maintaining his contact with his parents must be regarded as the first principle in the psychological care of the sick child, much else can be done for him. Nurses can be assigned to particular children to care for them in all ways, so that each child may feel he has a secure relationship with one real person. Wards can be small, both to make them feel homely and to permit of easy discipline, which is impossible to maintain in a friendly way with large groups of children. MacLennan [98] in discussing these matters emphasizes that there must be far more appreciation of child psychology amongst those administratively responsible for children's hospitals, and that it should be some one person's business to provide for the emotional needs of each child. Speaking of discipline, she remarks : " punishment is rarely necessary at all, if the nurses have the time and the knowledge to investigate the situation properly, and if they do not go in such fear of higher authority that they themselves become tyrannical." She recommends experiments in organizing staff and children in family groups, a theme which Spence [132] develops in his recommendations for the reform of long-stay hospitals :

" It would be better if the children lived in small groups under a house-mother, and from there went to their lessons in a school, to their treatment in a sick-bay, and to their entertainment in a central hall. There would be no disadvantage in the house-mother having had a nursing training, but that in itself is not the qualification for the work she will do. Her duty is to live with her group of children and attempt to provide the things of which they have been deprived."

It is necessary to emphasize that these principles apply with equal force to convalescent-homes and to psychiatric units for children. If young children are to get the benefits of convalescence without the ill effects of maternal deprivation they must be sent to homes which accept both mothers and children, as recommended for a different reason in chapter 9 (see page 87). Older children must not be sent so far away that parents cannot easily visit them, while their organization in ' family ' groups under house-mothers should become accepted practice. Unfortunately, psychiatric units for children are themselves still too often patterned on the old hospital plan of gigantic wards and impersonal corridors. Such units should be situated in buildings like ordinary large houses and run on hostel lines.

Finally, let the reader reflect for a moment on the astonishing practice which has been followed in maternity wards—of separating mothers and babies immediately after birth—and ask himself whether this is the way to promote a close mother-child relationship. It is to be hoped that this aberration of Western society will never be copied by the so-called less-developed countries !

CHAPTER 15

ADMINISTRATION OF CHILD-CARE SERVICES, AND PROBLEMS FOR RESEARCH

Administration of Child-Care Services

" First and last, our concern is with the family as an important primary group, of which the child is or was a part ". Any administrative structure which fails to recognize this is in danger of doing more harm than good. That this is so is testified by the authors of two of the most thorough surveys of foster-placement, both conducted in the USA. The authors of the above quotation, Healy et al.,[77] conclude :

" The failure of agencies, both public and private, as also of juvenile courts, training schools, etc., to lay proper stress on the fact that they are dealing with individuals who are members of families, is one answer to the question why much of the work done for these children is unsuccessful ".

Ten years later, Baylor & Monachesi [12] write :

" A notable weakness in the work of child-placing agencies is the lack of constructive case work with the families of the children concerned. The findings of this study furnish ample evidence of this. Delay in the return of children to their own homes may be the result, or, even more disastrous, the permanent separation of parents and children " (page 51).

Yet, though those agencies which deal only with limited aspects of the problem must be regarded as anachronisms, for historical reasons this is still too often the pattern. In most Western countries the care of neglected and homeless children has grown up piecemeal, in the face of public apathy, as the result of the single-minded energies of a few devoted people. A multitude of private charities has thus arisen, originally devoted to providing food and shelter for children who might otherwise have died. Though the result is patchy and inadequate, this record should not be forgotten, and in criticizing the way in which these ancient charities and large institutions have been run, the devoted service they have given while the public at large stood idly by must be remembered.

In most Western countries, recent decades have seen a clear trend towards the merging of agencies and the setting-up of consolidated services. In the USA, family welfare agencies and child-placing agencies have some-times been united. Describing the effects of this in St. Louis, Alt (quoted by Baylor & Monachesi [12]) writes :

" There has been an enrichment of the point of view of the family agency's staff expressed in an increased awareness of issues involved in the foster care of children.

Within the children's agency we see an appreciation of the possibilities of work with families which have been previously regarded as hopeless. The experience of the year... has indicated the possibilities of a more productive division of labor between workers with families and workers with children, which might not otherwise have been attained until many years later " (pages 53, 54).

Unfortunately, this merging of child-placing services and family services has not always occurred in the welfare states. For instance, in Great Britain, where, as a result of governmental authorities taking responsibility for the homeless child, there has been a great revolution in the child-care services, they still remain more or less divorced from family services. This is the direct result of the Curtis Committee, whose advice the Government accepted, having been confined to considering the symptoms—homeless children—and having been, by its restricted terms of reference, curbed from studying the more profound social disturbances lying behind these symptoms. As a result, in the United Kingdom, a confused situation persists in which no one authority has clear responsibility for preventing the neglect or ill-treatment of children in their own homes or of preventing family failure. Yet, as all administrators know and as the Curtis Committee itself recognized in its restricted field, divided responsibility is synonymous with inaction.

Thus the two first lessons to be drawn from these experiences are :

(a) Family welfare and child welfare are the two sides of a single coin and must be planned together.

(b) Responsibility for both must be clearly defined and unified.

A third principle which has been touched on many times is that :

(c) Family and child welfare is a skilled profession for which workers must be thoroughly trained.

A child-care service should be first and foremost a service giving skilled help to parents, including problem parents, to enable them to provide a stable and happy family life for their children. As subsidiary services, it will care for the unmarried mother and help her either to make a home for the child or arrange for his adoption, help mobilize relatives or neighbours to act as substitutes in an emergency, provide short-term care in necessary cases, while working towards the resumption of normal home life, and finally provide long-term care where all else fails. Only if it has legal and financial powers to do all these things, together with social workers equipped to put them into effect, can a service discharge its functions efficiently. As regards staff, it will require specialists as well as general practitioners—specialists in rehabilitating problem families, specialists in adoption, specialists in long-term care, to name but a few—but it would be a mistake for specialism to be carried too far or for each type of specialist to lose touch with the others. For all are concerned with the same essential problem and all are dependent on the same fundamental sciences—sociology and the psychology of human relations. By working together as partners in a family and child-care service, an integration of thought and practice can be achieved.

In all these respects the recommended trend may be likened to the trend which medicine has followed over the past centuries. Initially there was piecemeal charitable provision for the sick and needy, often little more than custodial in character, though as time progressed treatment for established conditions was added. The great revolution in medicine did not occur, however, until the causes of certain illnesses came to be known and broad preventive measures became possible. Though therapeutic and preventive medicine are still too often divorced from each other, there is a growing recognition of the need for integrated health services, the administrative responsibility for which is being vested largely in professional workers trained in the medical and allied sciences. It is to be hoped that progress in family and child welfare will follow a similar course. Where voluntary agencies are at present giving only a part of these services, especially where they are providing care for children away from home while taking no steps to prevent their removal or to reconstruct the family, they should consider a radical revision of their programme. Where government services are planned, it is imperative that they should be comprehensive and be given full responsibility for helping children within their families as well as outside them.

Throughout, this report has stressed the cardinal significance of maternal care for the preservation of mental health. It is, therefore, apparent that family and child-care services must in future be closely associated not only with each other but with mental health services ; for the ultimate aims of all three are identical, their techniques are growing more alike, their activities are becoming inextricably intertwined, and each is able greatly to aid the others. In countries which have not already differentiated health services from family and child welfare services—a pattern which characterizes certain well-developed countries of Western Europe, as well as less-developed countries—there is much to be gained from retaining all these services within one department. In many countries, however, where differentiation is already far advanced, this unification is barely possible. In either circumstance the mental health worker and the child-care worker must learn to work together. For this to be effective, changes will often be required in both. Not only is it necessary for child-care workers to be as proficient in the principles of mental health as they already are in the principles of physical hygiene, but mental health workers must take the trouble to learn far more than they now know about the problems of families and children and about the work of those concerned with their welfare. Only if a psychiatrist, a psychologist, or a psychiatric social worker is really familiar with day-to-day conditions is his advice likely to be useful. It is for this reason that the best work is now being done by family and child welfare agencies which have as staff members workers trained in mental health or which have been wise and fortunate enough to appoint psychiatric consultants who give much time and thought to the work. Only by such constant co-operative effort towards a common goal is it possible to develop the mutual respect and understanding necessary for success. The occasional referral of isolated cases to a psychiatrist busy with other problems is futile and apt to breed ill-will on both sides.

In this connexion may be noted the principles which the Lasker Mental Hygiene and Child Guidance Centre in Jerusalem is striving to follow in providing a mental hygiene service for immigrant children in Israel. The principal duties of the mental health worker are to help the staffs of the institutions to understand the disturbed children and themselves to act as therapeutic agents.

" The application of the principles of mental hygiene... demand not the setting-up of great numbers of sheltered environments and elaborate services for intensive work with individuals, but rather a scientific effort to adjust the greatest possible number of children in the existing environment, or rather, the adjustment of the environment to the child with emotional problems, by imparting or developing in the community insight and tolerance in respect of such problems. The great advantage of this approach is that it benefits not only the individual child, but all the children in the community, and therefore combines a therapeutic with a preventive function " (Caplan, personal communication).

As an instance of the success of this approach, an incident is described in which a group discussion of one case of bedwetting produced altered handling and symptomatic ' cure ' of a number of similar cases in the same institution. Such events, resulting from the combined operations of child-care and mental health workers, illustrations of which could be found in several other countries, lead to mutual understanding and real partnership. These conditions are essential, moreover, not only for good work but for fruitful research.

Research into Methods of Preventing Maternal Deprivation

There is hardly a topic touched on in the second part of this report around which there is not a shroud of ignorance. Here and there, thanks to the patient and painstaking work of an individual, there is a chink of light, but for most of the time the investigator must fumble in the dark, guided, if lucky, by the carefully formulated but unverified hypotheses of the observant worker, and at the worst confused by crystallized tradition and unwitting prejudice. These are not the conditions which make for effective and economic measures for preventing deprivation in childhood, nor are they the conditions which have led to the triumphs of the sister-science of preventive medicine. There will be no triumphs in preventive mental hygiene to compare with diphtheria immunization or malaria control without sustained and systematic research carried on over a long period and in many countries.

Though much of this research will necessarily be applied and operational in character, there are certain basic hypotheses which need testing ; the first being that the grown-up's capacity for parenthood is dependent in high degree on the parental care which he received in his childhood. If this proves true, with its corollary that neglected children grow up to become neglectful parents, understanding of the problem will be far advanced. Speaking of the great significance of this theory in understanding adjustment in marriage, Burgess & Cottrell [36] have remarked : " Its validation would greatly simplify the understanding of a great field of behaviour that otherwise seems to be hopelessly complex, complicated and often contradictory." In an understanding of maladjustment in marriage, of problem parents, promiscuity, and illegitimacy, with all their attendant neglect and rejection of children, this hypothesis is basic.

Even when it is proven true, however, as all the evidence at present suggests it will be, there remain many other factors—economic, social, and medical—which lead to children becoming deprived. As regards the social aspect, basic studies are required on the different patterns of family life and association, especially the forces which cause some families to live as isolated units unconnected with relatives and neighbours, and others to become parts of larger social groupings from which they get, and to which they give, support. In the analysis of these forces it is likely that comparative studies would be fruitful, both as between different cultures and as between subcultures of the same community.

In addition to these basic studies in personality development and social dynamics, the results of which might be expected to hold true for all societies, surveys are required in each community to determine the number of children suffering from deprivation and the nature and relative influence of each of the known factors. Such surveys would seek to elicit (a) the causes of the natural home group being unable to provide care for the children, and (b) the reasons why relatives are unable to act as substitutes. To be useful they would need to be as detailed as the schedule set out in Appendix 4, and to cover, moreover, all the children in the community and not merely those who had come to the notice of the authorities or agencies, since, unless they did so, children neglected in their own homes and children living with relatives would be excluded. Their conduct—to take account of the age of the child, the social and economic class of the parents, and similar variables—requires technical skill in survey methods as well as in social case-work, medicine, and sociology. For these reasons they would probably need to be undertaken by a university or a government department.

The carrying-out of such surveys in different communities and contrasting parts of the same community should be regarded as priority tasks since on their results will depend an understanding of the forces at work and the ordering of priorities for preventive action.

Research is also urgently required into the most suitable method of caring for children outside their own homes. Only by constant evaluation of their outcome can confidence be had in methods, and it is sad to reflect that, since the study of Theis 25 years ago, there have been few large-scale follow-ups of children brought up outside their own homes. The League of Nations Committee [90] found cause to bemoan this sorry state of affairs.

"Although twenty-five countries [in replying to the questionnaire regarding the results of boarding in families] stated that, on the whole, the system had been satisfactory, such a statement is too general to be accepted as representing the opinion of all or even a considerable proportion of those engaged in the work. Statistics of its extent and critical judgment based on observation and study of achievements, especially in relation to other types of child care, will be needed before an estimate can be made" (volume 2, page 10).

It is hoped that this neglect will be speedily rectified and that voluntary agencies and government departments will compete with each other to provide the most accurate and comprehensive data.

Unfortunately, there are serious technical difficulties in assessing the degree of success attending different methods of care. Apart from the great number of variables of which account must perforce be taken, there is the difficulty of finding reliable criteria of success or failure. This report has many times pointed to the apparent adjustment of children in institutions or foster-homes which has been belied by subsequent events. One notorious psychopathic English murderer was, while receiving training in an Approved School, so highly regarded that he was made the equivalent of head boy! Short-term overt behaviour cannot, therefore, be accepted as a satisfactory criterion. Instead it is necessary to use (a) psychological tests which reveal personality at a more profound level, e.g., the Rorschach, and (b) long-term follow-up studies. In using the follow-up method, the 15 criteria of social adjustment elaborated by Curle & Trist [49] would be appropriate and valuable. Especially relevant are those concerned with the individual's skill as marriage partner and parent, since there is so much reason to fear that present methods of caring for children away from home fail in this all-important respect.

Lastly, it must be recognized that not only is research difficult, but there is often active or passive resistance to its being undertaken. Hopkirk,[78] with long experience in the problem, notes that : "Trustees and executives are inclined to protect the work which they have established and the traditions which they have inherited and cherished" (page 208). As a result, difficulties, real and imaginary, are elaborated—conditions, it is said, have changed since these children were cared for ; it is unfair to submit them to an inquisitorial follow-up ; and in any case, remember, they were of bad heredity ! These defensive arguments, the invalidity of which has been demonstrated, are the result of fear, a fear which springs from the expectation that the research worker will be no more than a hostile critic.

The solution, of course, lies in the social scientist occupying a collaborative role in the agency, a role which the field workers accept as likely to lead to the greater understanding of their problems and the greater effectiveness of their work.

———————

CONCLUSION

The proper care of children deprived of a normal home life can now be seen to be not merely an act of common humanity, but to be essential for the mental and social welfare of a community. For, when their care is neglected, as happens in every country of the Western world today, they grow up to reproduce themselves. Deprived children, whether in their own homes or out of them, are a source of social infection as real and serious as are carriers of diphtheria and typhoid. And just as preventive measures have reduced these diseases to negligible proportions, so can determined action greatly reduce the number of deprived children in our midst and the growth of adults liable to produce more of them.

Yet, so far, no country has tackled this problem seriously. Even in so-called advanced countries there is a tolerance for conditions of bad mental hygiene in nurseries, institutions, and hospitals to a degree which, if paralleled in the field of physical hygiene, would long since have led to public outcry. The break-up of families and the shunting of illegitimates are accepted without demur. The twin problems of neglectful parents and deprived children are viewed fatalistically and left to perpetuate themselves. It seems probable that the main reasons for this fatalism are three in number : the assumption that a large proportion of these children are orphans and have no relatives ; an economic system which from time to time creates unrelieved poverty on a scale so great that social workers are powerless to help ; and a lack of understanding of psychiatric factors and a consequent impotence in managing cases where they predominate. In many Western countries, however, these three conditions no longer hold, but two others remain which hinder progress. In the first place, there is still a woeful scarcity of social workers skilled in the ability to diagnose the presence of psychiatric factors and to deal with them effectively. From what has been said hitherto, it is evident that unless a social worker has a good understanding of unconscious motivation she will be powerless to deal with many an unmarried mother, many a home which is in danger of breaking up, and many a case of conflict between parent and child. A particularly impressive feature of the past decade has been the extent to which the psycho-analytic approach to case-work has developed in the American schools of social work and the extent to which social agencies are employing child psychiatrists to aid their case-workers. Nevertheless, despite these hopeful signs, there is a tremendous task before all countries to train social workers in appropriate methods and child psychiatrists to aid them.

The second factor which still operates is a lack of conviction on the part of governments, social agencies, and the public that mother-love in infancy and childhood is as important for mental health as are vitamins and proteins for physical health. This lack of conviction has two roots —emotional and intellectual. A strong prejudice against believing it is not infrequently found in people who are heatedly preoccupied by the alleged inadequacy of children's own parents and who have a conspicuous need, of which they are not always aware, to prove themselves better able to look after the children than can their own parents. Members of committees, too, in contemplating the fruits of their labours, are apt to find more personal satisfaction in visiting an institution and reviewing a docile group of physically well cared for children than in trying to imagine the same children, rather more grubby perhaps, happily playing in their own or foster-homes. One must beware of a vested interest in the institutional care of children !

The intellectual doubts are more easily dealt with and may perhaps have been influenced by the scientific data reviewed in Part I of this report.

To those charged with preventive action the present position may be likened to that facing their predecessors responsible for public health a century ago. Theirs was a great opportunity for ridding their countries of dirt-borne diseases ; some took it, others remained hypercritical of the evidence and inert. True, the evidence presented in this report is at many points faulty, many gaps remain unfilled, and critical information is often missing ; but it must be remembered that evidence is never complete, that knowledge of truth is always partial, and that to await certainty is to await eternity. Let it be hoped, then, that all over the world men and women in public life will recognize the relation of mental health to maternal care, and will seize their opportunities for promoting courageous and far-reaching reforms.

APPENDICES

APPENDIX 1

VARIOUS RETROSPECTIVE STUDIES RELATING MENTAL ILLNESS
TO DEPRIVATION AND BROKEN HOMES

In the main text, reference has been made to some of the most significant retrospective studies relating mental illness, especially psychopathic personality, to maternal deprivation. There are a great number of other studies, the conclusions of which, either explicitly or implicitly, are the same. A few of these are noted here.

In discussing his general thesis regarding the interrelation of the affectionless character, persistent delinquency, and prolonged separation of child from mother, Bowlby [26, 27] remarks that he is a little astonished to find how lightly early separations had been treated by most workers in his field. Burt,[41] for example, placed these early separations among the minor factors in the origin of delinquency. His actual figures hardly warranted such a conclusion. Thus he had found that 23.5% of the boys and 36.5% of the girls had suffered prolonged absence from their parents. This contrasted with figures of 1.5% and 0.5% respectively for the controls. The results of investigations into broken homes were usually useless for comparison for reasons already given. Two investigations were worth mentioning, however, because they both illustrated the great importance of disturbances during the early years. In one of the investigations by Glueck & Glueck [59] the age of the child when the break in the family occurred was given. Out of 966 juvenile delinquents, 429 had come from broken homes. In 40% of the 429 (about 19% of the total) the break had occurred before the child was five years old. A similar analysis by Armstrong [5] had given comparable results. Of 660 runaway children, 29% had their homes broken before the age of four, and a further 28% between four and six years. Of 30 ' incorrigibles ', 12 (40%) had suffered broken homes before they were four years and a further 6 between the ages of four and six years.

Further indirect evidence is afforded by the research of East & Hubert.[51] Out of 26 cases illustrative of Borstal boys and adolescent prisoners who appeared specially difficult and either would not profit or had not profited by training, exactly half had probably suffered early separations. Details are not given of all the cases and the actual proportion may have been higher.

Powdermaker et al.[117] found that of 81 delinquent girls aged between 12 and 16, 33 (or 40%) came from broken homes.

Two elaborate studies of delinquency made in Sweden in the past decade point in the same direction. In both cases the sample has the defect of being concerned only with children who had been removed from home, the decision to do which may have been due as much to the bad home conditions as to the character of the child. Ahnsjö[1] found that, of 1,663 girls committed to institutions for delinquency in the years 1903-1937, only 75% were looked after by both parents at the time of their birth, and that the homes of nearly half of the remainder were broken through divorce or the death of one or both parents at the time the child was admitted to the institution. Largely no doubt as a result of these conditions, very many of the children had lived with more than one set of relatives or foster-parents in the course of their lives. In the case of 550 in detention homes for severe and abnormal cases, admitted at an average age of about 16 years, no less than 30% had experienced such changes and separations.

Otterström,[112] in her study of 1,315 boys and 300 girls who had either required special educational measures on account of delinquency or had been convicted of crimes, found that in the case of 42% of the boys and 65% of the girls the homes were broken when the child was admitted (inclusive of children whose parents were neither married nor cohabiting at the time of their birth).

Findings similar to those of Ahnsjö and Otterström emerge from the survey of children in hostels for difficult children who had been evacuated from the cities of Great Britain during the late war.[75] They comprised over 400 children (80% boys, 20% girls), aged between 6 and 14, the great majority of whom were in the hostels on account of stealing or being otherwise unmanageable, or for enuresis. Of 418 children about whose homes something was known, no less than 45% came from broken homes —one or both parents dead, a parent deserted, or the child illegitimate. Of the remainder nearly one half (about 25% of the whole) came from homes where, although the parents were living together, conditions were very bad, including cruelty, immorality, mental instability, unhappy family relationships, neglect and harsh treatment, and rejection. Only 30% came from homes which were complete and reasonably happy.

Bowlby [26, 27] has discussed the probability of affectionless characters being responsible for sexual offences. Evidence of this connexion comes from several sources. In the League of Nations study of prostitutes,[89] the findings were as follows :

" Apart from the small percentage who were illegitimate, in most of the lists between one-fifth and one-third had lost one parent through death or separation while they were still young. In addition, the percentage brought up in institutions, by foster-parents or relatives, is 20% or more in four lists, and over 10% in thirteen of the sixteen lists which give information on this point " (page 31).

This general picture is confirmed by Safier et al.[127] who have studied some hundreds of promiscuous men and women :

" About 60% of both the men and women came from broken homes occasioned by death, separation, or divorce. In the case of one-half of all the men the home was broken before the age of 13, and for one-third before the age of 7. The median age for the break-up of the home for those whose homes were broken was age 6 ... Among the patients whose homes had been broken, it was not unusual for the patient to have been placed in boarding schools, foster homes, institutions, or in the homes of relatives. A number of the patients had had a series of such placements. Some patients had had no care by either parent from birth or shortly thereafter. Some of these had been born out of wedlock. In other instances one or both parents had remarried and the patients were reared in homes with stepfathers or stepmothers... Conflicts were most pronounced in the cases where the family life had been unstable and the patient had been entrusted to the care of first one person and then another."

A small sample of 50 promiscuous males examined by Bundesen et al.[35] confirms these findings, 56% showing evidence of abnormal childhood conditions.

Studies of neurosis among soldiers in the second World War also revealed the high incidence among them of broken homes. Thus McGregor,[97] in analysing the findings in 2,228 consecutive patients admitted to a military hospital for neurosis, found that 48% formed a personality group having the traits of timidity, immaturity, dependence, and frustration. " They came from broken homes or homes where there had been much emotional stress in early life. On the whole, this group revealed marked evidence of love-deprivation in childhood." Madow & Hardy[99] confirmed this. Of 211 soldiers suffering from war neurosis, 36% came from homes which had been broken before the patients were 16.

Even with schizophrenics broken homes are a common and probably significant feature of the history. Pollock et al.[115] found a broken home in the history of 38% of 175 patients suffering from dementia praecox. Lidz & Lidz,[93] in studying 50 schizophrenics who had become psychotic before the age of 21 years, found an almost identical percentage—40%. These high figures for schizophrenics contrast with a figure of only 17% found by Pollock et al. for a group of 155 patients suffering from manic-depressive psychosis, a percentage little if at all above that of the ordinary population.

Another study, this time from Hungary, relates to accident proneness. In tracing the histories of 100 cases admitted to the surgical wards on account of recurrent accidents, Csillag & Hedri[48] found that no less than 54% had either lost their parents in childhood or had parents who were separated.

Finally, there is a study carried out by Mulock Houwer[106] in the Netherlands after the war of the home background of children found guilty of treason during it. Of 275 children, 52% came from broken homes.

For various reasons the figures given in these different studies are not strictly comparable, a special difficulty being divergences of practice regarding the inclusion or not of illegitimate children brought up by their mothers only. It is none the less useful to tabulate some of these figures. They are therefore set out in table XIX.

TABLE XIX.   INCIDENCE OF BROKEN HOMES AMONG PATIENTS SUFFERING FROM VARIOUS FORMS OF NEUROTIC DISABILITY

Author	Country	Nature of disability	Number of patients	Percentage from broken homes before the age of	
				6 years	16 years
Glueck & Glueck	USA	juvenile delinquency	966	19	44
Armstrong	USA	running away	660	57	
Powdermaker et al.	USA	delinquent girls	81		40
Ahnsjö	Sweden	delinquent girls	1,663		60
Otterström	Sweden	delinquent boys delinquent girls	1,315 300		42 65
Menut	France	children with behaviour disorders	839		66
Ministry of Health	England and Wales	maladjusted children	418		45
Safier et al.	USA	promiscuous men promiscuous women	255 } 365 }		60
Bundesen et al.	USA	promiscuous men	50		56
Madow & Hardy	USA	neurotic soldiers	211		36
Pollock et al.	USA	dementia praecox	175		38
Lidz & Lidz	USA	young schizophrenics	50		40
Csillag & Hedri	Hungary	accident proneness	100		54
Mulock Houwer	Netherlands	treason in children	275		52

Though it is unfortunate that most of these studies lack controls, such control figures as exist are consistent.   Menut [101] found the percentage of broken homes in his very large Parisian control group to be 12%, while Madow & Hardy [99] quote three different American sources which show the percentage to lie between 11 and 15. It seems virtually certain, therefore, that the incidence of broken homes in all these studies is significantly higher than would be found in a normal group drawn from any of the populations concerned.

Once again, of course, there is always the possibility of the results being due to heredity and not to environment. Often the home is broken because one or other parent is psychotic or psychopathic. May it not be that it is the bad genes inherited by the offspring which account for their turning out badly ? This is a matter which both Ahnsjö and Otterström discuss at length, though their own samples do not permit of their giving an answer.

Apart from the evidence already given dealing with this issue, there are two interesting studies by Barry regarding the incidence of bereavement in patients suffering from psychosis in adolescence or early adult life, which bear on it. In his earlier study,[9] concerned with 549 patients (306 male, 243 female) admitted between the ages of 16 and 25, he shows that, whereas the incidence of paternal deaths runs parallel with the incidence in the general population, the incidence of maternal deaths is significantly higher. (15.7% of his patients suffered the death of their mother before they were 12, in contrast to 5.3% of the general population.) The fact that death of mothers is frequent in such cases while that of fathers is not makes it virtually certain that hereditary factors are not the explanation of these data, but is, on the contrary, important confirmatory evidence of the central value to the small child of his relation to his mother and the emotional trauma which he sustains at her loss. In a later statistical study, Barry[10] concludes that the critical period for separation from the mother is before the age of eight years.

So far as is known there has been only one study which has set out to test the hypothesis that the broken home is an important factor in a child's development. This was carried out by Wallenstein,[145] who surveyed the whole school population of part of New York. Of 3,000 boys and girls, 550 were from broken homes. Over half the total were examined psychologically and careful comparisons were made, many of which showed the children from broken homes to have developed less favourably than the others. Wallenstein concludes quite rightly, however, that the concept of the broken home is not satisfactory for scientific purposes.

DIFFERENCES IN RORSCHACH RESPONSES BETWEEN INSTITUTION CHILDREN AND OTHERS

So far as is known only two workers have done systematic work with institution children using the Rorschach test—Loosli-Usteri in Geneva in the late 1920s, and Goldfarb in New York during the past decade.

Goldfarb's work [64] was undertaken on the same sample of children as that for which results in respect of other tests are presented in tables VI and VII. This consisted of 15 pairs of children who at the time of the examination ranged in age from 10 to 14 years. One group of 15 was in the institution from about 6 months of age to $3\frac{1}{2}$ years ; the other group had not had this experience. He found that the institution children did not differ from the controls in the number or location of the responses or in the main determinants (with the exception of C), which means that the quantity of output and the attempted methods of organizing perceptions

TABLE XX. DIFFERENCES IN RORSCHACH RESPONSES BETWEEN CHILDREN WHO HAD SPENT THEIR FIRST THREE YEARS IN AN INSTITUTION AND CONTROLS WHO HAD NOT (GOLDFARB)

Significance of response	Classification of response	Result expressed as	Results		
			Insti-tution group	control group	P
Loose perceptions poorly seen, arbitrary responses	W —	mean percentage scores	47	19	< .05
	F +		43	75	< .01
	O —		91	20	< .01
Confabulations and poor organization	Presence of DW	number of children showing responses	7	0	< .01
	Beck's Z score below 20		10	4	< .05
Lack of control over emotional responses	At least one C	" "	3	0	< .05
	CF + C > FC	" "	5	1	< .02
Diminished drive to social conformity	Less than three popular responses	" "	10	3	< .01
	Original responses	mean percentage scores	24	13	< .1

Note : Total number of children in each group is 15.

were similar. The two groups were also similar in their tendency to see movement, and animal and human percepts, and in their use of shading.

The two groups differed markedly, however, in the quality of their responses. For instance, while attempting similar perceptions, the institution children's responses were much less accurate and tended to have less relation to the blots. They tended to be poorly organized and often confabulated so that an idea suggested by one part of the blot would be extended arbitrarily to the whole, the resulting percept having little relation to the actual stimulus. A preponderance of pure colour responses—that is, responses determined solely by colour without being organized into any form, e.g., blood—demonstrated the poorer emotional control of the institution children. Moreover they showed few of the popular responses (i.e., those given by the majority of subjects) and a greater number of original ones, though the latter were poorly seen. This indicates that they were less in touch with reality and with popular modes of thought, and may also suggest a lack of social conformity. Most of these differences are summarized in table XX.

Goldfarb [68] also compared the institution children with schizophrenics of the same age. Rorschach responses were remarkably similar in many respects, the most evident difference being the relative absence of anxiety in the institution children and its presence to a profound degree in the schizophrenics.

Loosli-Usteri's work [94] was undertaken much earlier than Goldfarb's when different methods of Rorschach scoring were in use. The data presented are different and items which Goldfarb found to show significant differences were not used in the analysis. Moreover, the sample studied was different in respect of the children's institution experiences ; all the children were actually in the institution when studied, in contrast to Goldfarb's who were in foster-homes, and many had probably not spent their first three years in the institution as Goldfarb's had. The results of tests of the statistical significance of differences are not given. As a result, comparisons are not easily made, though several of Loosli-Usteri's findings appear to confirm Goldfarb's.

She compared a group of 21 boys aged 10 to 13 years from an institution in Geneva (length of time in the institution unstated) with 63 primary schoolboys of the same city who were living with their families. Like Goldfarb, she found that many of the institution children showed poor abstract ability—" their mode of thought is infantile and autistic ". She also found that there was an inverse relation between this feature and the presence of neurotic symptoms. The institution children were much more introverted than the controls, lacked emotional response, and tended to be depressed. They also showed a lower number of ' popular ' responses. In these respects the results confirm or are concordant with Goldfarb's. However, she did not find a lowered emotional control, while positive findings not mentioned by Goldfarb were a marked tendency to contra-suggestibility and a tendency of institution children with neurotic symptoms to refuse to give responses.

From this it may be inferred that Loosli-Usteri's sample was hetero-geneous in regard to institutional experience and that, while some of the children had been in the institution during their early years and had developed along psychopathic lines, others had entered the institution later and had developed reactions of a more neurotic kind. Nothing in Loosli-Usteri's data contradicts Goldfarb's conclusions. Her findings are some of the earliest to call attention to the high incidence of psychiatric disturbance among children in institutions.

NOTE ON GOLDFARB'S STUDY OF SOCIAL ADJUSTMENT IN RELATION TO AGE OF ENTRY TO AN INSTITUTION

Goldfarb [67] bases his views on the importance of deprivation in the first year of life on an interesting study carried out with his usual care. He took for his sample children aged 12 years and over (average age about $14\frac{1}{2}$) who had been in an institution for varying periods of time during their first three years of life. All these children were then assessed by case-workers for their present social adjustment. Omitting those of uncertain adjustment, he selected 15 pairs of children matched for age and sex, half of whom were socially well-adjusted and the other half severe problems. The majority had been consistent in their behaviour ever since being placed. Goldfarb then demonstrates that the differences in these children's behaviour cannot be accounted for by their heredity, or by the attitude of their parents or of their foster-parents. On the other hand, there was a significant difference between the groups in respect of the age of admission to the institution, the mean age of the well-adjusted being 10.9 months and that of the badly adjusted 5.8 months (P lies between 0.02 and 0.05).

Though the general importance of these figures is clear, it is unfortunate that Goldfarb has not given us his data in more detail since it is not easy to be certain of their precise significance. It does not appear that Goldfarb's own conclusion—that " the lasting importance of the first half year in the child's life is strikingly indicated "—is warranted, because the badly adjusted group were not in the institution for much of their first half year of life, the average age of entry being all but six months. No conclusions regarding the first half-year are therefore possible. The legitimate and very important conclusion appears to be that deprivation in the second half-year of the child's life has more far-reaching consequences than deprivation occurring later.

APPENDIX 4

NOTE ON STATISTICS REGARDING CAUSES OF CHILDREN
BEING TAKEN INTO CARE AWAY FROM HOME

The figures quoted in chapter 8 are based on seven studies from three different countries which happened to be readily available. It is not known how representative they are of the countries concerned and they are used here merely as pointers.

United Kingdom

(i) 1,195 children in the care of three county authorities in England, representing urban, semi-urban, and rural communities. Date 1945. Reported by Brockington.[29]

(ii) 346 children from 234 families in the care of a large voluntary agency (Dr. Barnardo's Homes). These cases are stated to represent about 10% of the 2,000 admissions to the Home between January 1937 and January 1940. Reported in *The neglected child and his family*.[110]

(iii) 500 children admitted to the care of another voluntary agency (National Children's Homes) in the years 1940-1941. Reported in the annual report for 1948.[109]

(iv) 51 children in the care of 12 different homes comprising all types of institution existing in Britain in 1946. Reported by Bodman et al.[24]

United States of America

(i) About 500 requests for help to a large private agency in New York in the year 1949 (not published).

(ii) 209 children discharged from foster-home care by the Maryland Children's Aid Society in 1940-1942.[100]

Sweden

73 children in the care of six homes, two long-term and four short-term, about 1946-1947. Reported by Thysell.[140]

Unfortunately the form in which the data are given is very varied. Often the state of the natural home group is not given explicitly, though in some instances it can be deduced. The underlying reasons for neglect, etc., are never shown, nor is any attention given to reasons for relatives being unable to act as substitutes.

— 170 —

The figures given in table XXI are believed to be tolerably accurate translations into a common form of the raw figures. Although in certain cases more information was available under the heading 'Natural home group not functioning effectively', it is not sufficiently detailed to be useful and has therefore been omitted.

TABLE XXI.   CAUSES OF CHILDREN BEING DEPRIVED OF A NORMAL HOME LIFE

Country	Sweden	United States of America		United Kingdom			
Investigation	Thysell	New York agency	Malone	Brockington	Dr. Barnardo's Homes	National Children's Homes	Bodman et al.
Number of children	73	500	209	1,195	346	500	52
Approximate date	1946-1947	1949	1942	1945	1937-1940	1940-1941	1946
	%	%	%	%	%	%	%
(a) Natural home group never established: illegitimacy	25	9	16	10	40	27	25
(b) Natural home group not functioning effectively:							
poverty or neglect by parents	40	4	16	60.5	31	(20)	—
maladjustment of child	3	26	18	0.5	—	(5)	—
(c) Natural home group broken up:							
death of one parent	1	5		7		(56)	25
death of both parents		1		3			
physical illness of parent	23	6	40	—	59	—	2
mental illness of parent		6		9		—	25
desertion, separation, divorce	5	21		10		—	23
(d) Others and unknown	3	22	10	—	—	—	—
	100	100	100	100	*	*	100

* Figures for these groups cannot be analysed so that the percentages total 100.

The great differences in these figures are due partly to a lack of uniformity in their presentation but probably more to real differences in the samples reflecting, almost certainly, radical differences in policy of admission. For instance, much will depend on whether aid is given to widows or relatives to help them care for children at home or whether all such children are collected and put in an orphanage.

One difficulty in the tabulations on this subject in existing publications is that data describing the present state of the home, e.g., neglect, cruelty, poverty, etc., are mixed up with more basic data referring to the state and capacity of parents. These are of course largely independent variables —neglect and poverty can characterize the home of an unmarried mother, a widow, and of parents living together. For this reason two main groups of data referring to the home are needed :

(1) Data referring to the presence or otherwise of an emergency situation requiring action.

(2) Data referring to the state of the natural home group.

Certain items, such as ' hospitalization of mother ' would appear in both categories (1) and (2) ; others, such as ' neglect ' or ' mental instability of father', would appear in only one (neglect in (1), instability in (2)).

In addition to these two groups, there are needed :

(3) Data referring to the availability or otherwise of aid from relatives.

The following is a rough draft of headings under each of these three main variables :

(1) Emergency situation
>   Mother dead
>   Mother in hospital
>   Mother in prison
>   Mother deserted
>   Immorality in home
>   Cruelty
>   Gross neglect
>   Family without house
>   Children found wandering or abandoned
>   No emergency

(2) State of natural home group
>   (a) Presence and capacity of father
>>   present and effective
>>   present but incapacitated by :
>>>   physical ill-health
>>>   mental ill-health
>>>   instability of character
>>>   mental defect
>>   absent on account of :
>>>   not being married to mother
>>>   death

hospitalization (physical)
hospitalization (mental)
mental defective colony
prison
desertion, separation, divorce
employment elsewhere

(b) Presence and capacity of mother
as for father, substituting ' full-time employment ' for
' employment elsewhere '

(3) Availability of aid from relatives

available from...

not available because of :

relatives dead, aged, or ill
relatives living far away
relatives unable to help for economic reasons
relatives unwilling to help
parents never had relatives

Only if data are given with this degree of detail can the problems to be faced be understood and effective measures be devised for meeting them.

BIBLIOGRAPHY

1. Ahnsjö, S. (1941) *Acta paediatr., Stockh.* **28**, Suppl. 3, 1
2. Aichhorn, A. (1925) *Verwahrloste Jugend*, Wien
3. Aichhorn, A. (1935) *Wayward youth*, New York (translation of 2)
4. Alt, H. (1951) *Amer. J. Orthopsychiat.* **21**, 105
5. Armstrong, C. P. (1932) *660 runaway boys*, Boston, Mass.
6. Baker, I. M. (1949) *Child Welfare*, **28**, May, p. 3
7. Bakwin, H. (1942) *Amer. J. Dis. Child.* **63**, 30
8. Bakwin, H. (1949) *J. Pediat.* **35**, 512
9. Barry, H., jr. (1939) *Amer. J. Orthopsychiat.* **9**, 355
10. Barry, H., jr. (1949) *Arch. Neurol. Psychiat.*, Chicago, **62**, 630
11. Bayley, N. (1933) *Mental growth during the first three years*, Worcester, Mass. (condensed report in : Barker, R. G., Kounin, J. S. & Wright, H. F., ed. (1943) *Child behavior and development*, New York)
12. Baylor, E. M. H. & Monachesi, E. D. (1939) *The rehabilitation of children : the theory and practice of child placement*, New York
13. Bender, L. (1946) *Child Study*, **23**, 74
14. Bender, L. (1947) *Psychopathic behavior disorders in children.* In : Lindner, R. M. & Seliger, R. V., ed. *Handbook of correctional psychology*, New York
15. Bender, L. & Yarnell, H. (1941) *Amer. J. Psychiat.* **97**, 1158
16. Beres, D. & Obers, S. J. (1949) *The effects of extreme deprivation in infancy on psychic structure in adolescence : a study in ego development* (unpublished paper read at annual meeting of the American Orthopsychiatric Association)
17. Bettelheim, B. & Sylvester, E. (1947) *Amer. J. Orthopsychiat.* **17**, 684
18. Bettelheim, B. & Sylvester, E. (1948) *Amer. J. Orthopsychiat.* **18**, 191
19. Binning, G. (1948) *Health*, Toronto, March
20. Binning, G. (1949) *Health*, Toronto, July/August, p. 10
21. Blacker, C. P. (1946) *Eugen. Rev.* **38**, 117
22. Blacker, C. P. (1946) *Neurosis and the mental health services*, Oxford
23. Bodman, F. (1950) *J. ment. Sci.* **96**, 245
24. Bodman, F., MacKinlay, M. & Sykes, K. (1950) *Lancet*, **1**, 173
25. Bowlby, J. (1940) *Int. J. Psycho-Anal.* **21**, 154
26. Bowlby, J. (1944) *Int. J. Psycho-Anal.* **25**, 19
27. Bowlby, J. (1946) *Forty-four juvenile thieves, their characters and homelife*, London (reprint of 26)
28. Bowlby, J. (1949) *Hum. Rel.* **2**, 123
29. Brockington, C. F. (1946) *Lancet*, **1**, 933
30. Brodbeck, A. J. & Irwin, O. C. (1946) *Child Develpm.* **17**, 145
31. Brosse, T. (1950) *Homeless children*, Paris (UNESCO)
32. Brosse, T. (1950) *War-handicapped children*, Paris (UNESCO)
33. Brown, F. (1937) *J. appl. Psychol.* **21**, 379
34. Bühler, C. (1935) *From birth to maturity*, London
35. Bundesen, H. N., Plotke, F. & Eisenberg, H. (1949) *Amer. J. publ. Hlth*, **39**, 1535
36. Burgess, E. W. & Cottrell, L. S., jr. (1939) *Predicting success or failure in marriage*, New York
37. Burlingham, D. & Freud, A. (1942) *Annual report of a residential war nursery*, London

38. Burlingham, D. & Freud, A. (1942) *Young children in wartime*, London
39. Burlingham, D. & Freud, A. (1943) *Infants without families*, London
40. Burlingham, D. & Freud, A. (1944) *Monthly report of Hampstead nurseries*, May (unpublished)
41. Burt, C. (1929) *The young delinquent*, London
42. Burt, C. (1940) *Brit. J. educ. Psychol.* **10**, 8
43. Carey-Trefzer, C. J. (1949) *J. ment. Sci.* **95**, 535
44. Clothier, F. (1948) *Nerv. Child,* **7**, 154
45. Corner, G. W. (1944) *Ourselves unborn*, New Haven
46. Cowan, E. A. & Stout, E. (1939) *Amer. J. Orthopsychiat.* **9**, 330
47. Croydon, County Borough of (1948-1949) *Report of Children's Officer*
48. Csillag, I. & Hedri, E., jr. (1949) *Industr. Med.* **18**, 29
49. Curle, A. & Trist, E. L. (1947) *Hum. Rel.* **1**, 240
50. Durfee, H. & Wolf, K. (1933) *Z. Kinderforsch.* **42**, 273
51. East, N. W. & Hubert, W. H. de B. (1939) *The psychological treatment of crime*, London
52. Edelston, H. (1943) *Genet. Psychol. Monogr.* **28**, 1
53. Embry, M. (1937) *Planning for the unmarried mother*, New York
54. Family Service Association of America (1950) *Diagnosis and treatment of marital problems*, New York
55. Fitzgerald, O. (1948) *J. ment. Sci.* **94**, 701
56. Fried, R. & Mayer, M. F. (1948) *J. Pediat.* **33**, 444
57. Gesell, A. & Amatruda, C. (1947) *Developmental diagnosis : normal and abnormal child development. Clinical methods and pediatric applications*, 2nd ed. New York
58. Gindl, I., Hetzer, H. & Sturm, M. (1937) *Z. angew. Psychol.* **52**, 310
59. Glueck, S. & Glueck, E. T. (1934) *One thousand juvenile delinquents*, Cambridge, Mass.
60. Goldfarb, W. (1943) *Amer. J. Orthopsychiat.* **13**, 249
61. Goldfarb, W. (1943) *Child Develpm.* **14**, 213
62. Goldfarb, W. (1943) *J. exp. Educ.* **12**, 106
63. Goldfarb, W. (1944) *Amer. J. Orthopsychiat.* **14**, 162
64. Goldfarb, W. (1944) *Amer. J. Orthopsychiat.* **14**, 441
65. Goldfarb, W. (1945) *Amer. J. Orthopsychiat.* **15**, 247
66. Goldfarb, W. (1945) *Amer. J. Psychiat.* **102**, 18
67. Goldfarb, W. (1947) *Amer. J. Orthopsychiat.* **17**, 449
68. Goldfarb, W. (1949) *Amer. J. Orthopsychiat.* **19**, 624
69. Goldstein, K. & Scheerer, M. (1941) *Psychol. Monogr.* **53**, 151
70. Gordon, H. L. (1949) *Foster care for children.* In : *Social Work Year Book*, New York, p. 211
71. Gordon, H. L. (1950) *Child Welfare,* **29**, January, p. 3
72. Great Britain, Care of Children Committee (1946) *Report ... presented by the Secretary of State for the Home Department, the Minister of Health and the Minister of Education*, London (Curtis Report)
73. Great Britain, Home Office (1949) *Reception centres. Memorandum ... for the guidance of local authorities ...*, London
74. Great Britain, Ministry of Health (1943) *The care of illegitimate children*, London (Circular No. 2866, rev.)
75. Great Britain, Ministry of Health (1944) *Hostels for ' difficult ' children. A survey of experience under the evacuation scheme*, London
76. Great Britain, Ministry of Health (1948) *Children and the British Government evacuation scheme*, London
77. Healy, W., Bronner, A. F., Baylor, E. M. H. & Murphy, J. P. (1929) *Reconstructing behavior in youth : a study of problem children in foster families*, New York

78. Hopkirk, H. W. (1944) *Institutions serving children*, New York
79. Hunt, J. McV. (1941) *J. abnorm. soc. Psychol.* **36**, 338
80. Hutchinson, D. (1943) *In quest of foster parents : a point of view on homefinding*, New York
81. Isaacs, S., ed. (1941) *The Cambridge evacuation survey*, London
82. Isaacs, S. (1948) *Children in institutions*. In : *Childhood and after*, London, p. 208
83. Jewish Board of Guardians (1950) *Methods and preliminary findings of total population study at Hawthorne-Cedar Knolls School*, New York (unpublished)
84. Jolowicz, A. R. (1946) *The hidden parent : some effects of the concealment of the parents' life upon the child's use of a foster home* (paper given at the New York State Conference on Social Welfare)
85. Jones, M. C. & Burks, B. S. (1936) *Personality development in childhood*, Washington, D.C. (Society for Research in Child Development, Monographs, **1**, No. 4)
86. Klein, M. (1948) *A contribution to the psychogenesis of manic-depressive states.* In : *Contributions to psycho-analysis, 1921-1945*, London, p. 282
87. Kline, D. & Overstreet, H. M. (1948) *Soc. Serv. Rev.* **22**, 324
88. *Lancet*, 1949, **1**, 975
89. League of Nations (1938) *Prostitutes : their early lives*, Geneva
90. League of Nations (1938) *The placing of children in families*, Geneva, 2 vol.
91. Levy, D. (1937) *Amer. J. Psychiat.* **94**, 643
92. Levy, R. J. (1947) *J. Personal.* **15**, 233
93. Lidz, R. W. & Lidz, T. (1949) *Amer. J. Psychiat.* **106**, 332
94. Loosli-Usteri, M. (1929) *Arch. Psychol.* **22**, 51
95. Loosli-Usteri, M. (1948) *New Era*, **29**, 1
96. Lowrey, L. G. (1940) *Amer. J. Orthopsychiat.* **10**, 576
97. McGregor, H. G. (1944) *J. Neurol. Neurosurg. Psychiat.* **7**, 21
98. MacLennan, B. W. (1949) *Lancet*, **2**, 209
99. Madow, L. & Hardy, S. E. (1947) *Amer. J. Orthopsychiat.* **17**, 521
100. Malone, B. (1942) *Children away from home*, Baltimore (Maryland Children's Aid Society)
101. Menut, G. (1943) *La dissociation familiale et les troubles du caractère chez l'enfant*, Paris
102. Mersham Children's Reception Centre (1948) *Interim report*, Mersham, Kent
103. Michaels, R. & Brenner, R. F. *A follow-up study of adoptive homes*, New York (Child Adoption Committee of the Free Synagogue) (unpublished)
104. Montefiore Hospital, New York (1949) *Home care : origin, organization and present status of the extra-mural program of Montefiore Hospital*, New York
105. Morlock, M. & Campbell, H. (1946) *Maternity homes for unmarried mothers : a community service*, Washington, D.C. (US Department of Labor, Children's Bureau Publication 309)
106. Mulock Houwer, D. Q. R. (1947) *Enige aspecten betreffende het probleem der jeugdige politieke delinquenten*, Amsterdam
107. Mumford, L. (1944) *Condition of man*, London
108. Murphy, L. B. (1937) *Social behavior and child personality*, New York (condensed report in : Barker, R. G., Kounin, J. S. & Wright, H. F., ed. (1943) *Child behavior and development*, New York)
109. National Children's Homes (1948) *Annual report*, London
110. National Council of Social Service (1948) *The neglected child and his family*, Oxford
111. Orgel, S. Z. (1941) *Amer. J. Orthopsychiat.* **11**, 371
112. Otterström, E. (1946) *Delinquency and children from bad homes : a study of prognosis from a social point of view*, Lund
113. Pickerill, C. & Pickerill, H. P. (1947) *Nurs. Mirror*, August
114. Piquer y Jover, J. J. (1946) *El niño abandonado y delincuente*, Madrid

115. Pollock, H. M., Malzberg, B. & Fuller, R. G. (1939) *Hereditary and environmental factors in the causation of manic-depressive psychoses and dementia praecox*, Utica, N.Y.
116. Pollock, J. C. & Rose, J. A. (1949) *Child Welfare*, **28**, June, p. 3
117. Powdermaker, F., Levis, H. T. & Touraine, G. (1937) *Amer. J. Orthopsychiat.* **7**, 58
118. Querido, A. (1946) *Med. Offr*, **75**, 193
119. Rheingold, H. L. (1943) *Amer. J. Orthopsychiat.* **13**, 41
120. Ribble, M. (1943) *The rights of infants : early psychological needs and their satisfaction*, New York
121. Richman, L. H. (1946) *Soc. Serv. Rev.* **20**, 354
122. Richman, L. H. (1948) *Child*, **13**, No. 1, p. 8
123. Ripin, R. (1933) *Psychol. Bull.* **30**, 680
124. Robinson, J. F. (1947) *Amer. J. Psychiat.* **103**, 814
125. Rome, R. (1939) *A study of some factors entering into the unmarried mother's decision regarding the disposition of her child* (Smith College School for Social Work : unpublished thesis)
126. Roudinesco, J. & Appell, G. (1950) *Sem. Hôp. Paris*, **26**, 2271
127. Safier, B., Corrigan, H. G., Fein, E. J. & Bradway, K. P. (1949) *A psychiatric approach to the treatment of promiscuity*, New York
128. Savage, S. W. (1946) *Brit. med. J.* **1**, 86
129. Sharp, J. (1950) *Nurs. Times*, **46**, 152
130. Simonsen, K. M. (1947) *Examination of children from children's homes and day nurseries*, Copenhagen
131. Spence, J. C. (1946) *The purpose of the family : a guide to the care of children*, London
132. Spence, J. C. (1947) *Brit. med. J.* **1**, 125
133. Spitz, R. A. (1945) *Hospitalism : an inquiry into the genesis of psychiatric conditions in early childhood* [I]. In : *The psychoanalytic study of the child*, **1**, 53
134. Spitz, R. A. & Wolf, K. M. (1946) *Anaclitic depression : an inquiry into the genesis of psychiatric conditions in early childhood* [II]. In : *The psychoanalytic study of the child*, **2**, 313
135. Spitz, R. A. & Wolf, K. M. (1946) *Genet. Psychol. Monogr.* **34**, 57
136. Stern, E. M. & Hopkirk, H. W. (1947) *The housemother's guide*, New York
137. Stott, D. H. (1950) *Delinquency and human nature*, Dunfermline
138. Terman, L. M. (1938) *Psychological factors in marital happiness*, New York
139. Theis, S. van S. (1924) *How foster children turn out*, New York (State Charities Aid Association Publication No. 165)
140. Thysell, T. (1948) *Sociala Meddelanden*, **58**, 851
141. Tibout, N. H. C. (1948) In : *International Congress on Mental Health, London, 1948*, **2**, 46
142. Toronto & District, Welfare Council of (1943) *A study of the adjustment of teen age children born out of wedlock who remained in the custody of their mothers or relatives*, Toronto
143. United Nations Economic and Social Council (1948) *Economic and Social Council. Official Records : Third Year, Seventh Session. Supplement No. 8. Report of the Social Commission*, New York, pp. 28, 29
144. Vulliamy, C. (1944) *Self-government.* In : *Children's communities*, London (New Education Fellowship Monograph No. 1, p. 10)
145. Wallenstein, N. (1937) *Character and personality of children from broken homes*, New York
146. Watkins, A. G. & Lewis-Faning, E. (1949) *Brit. med. J.* **2**, 616
147. Wetzel, N. C. (1948) *Treatment of growth failure in children : an application of the grid technique*, Cleveland

148. Willesden, Borough of (1939) *Annual Health Report for 1939*, Willesden, Middlesex
149. Wilson, A. T. M. (1949) *Hum. Rel.* **2**, 233
150. Winnicott, D. W. & Britton, C. (1944) *The problem of homeless children.* In : *Children's communities*, London (New Education Fellowship Monograph No. 1, p. 1)
151. Winnicott, D. W. & Britton, C. (1947) *Hum. Rel.* **1**, 87
152. Wittkower, E. D. (1948) *Brit. J. vener. Dis.* **24**, 59
153. Wofinden, R. C. (1944) *Publ. Hlth, Lond.* **57**, 136
154. Wofinden, R. C. (1946) *Eugen. Rev.* **38**, 127
155. Wolkonir, B. (1947) *Child Welfare League of America Bulletin*, **26**, 1
156. Wollen, C. A. (1949) *The relationship between the child guidance service and centres for short-term observation of children* (unpublished paper read to the British Psychological Society)
157. World Health Organization, Expert Committee on Mental Health (1950) *World Hlth Org. techn. Rep. Ser.* **9**, 7
158. Young, L. R. (1947) *Personality patterns in unmarried mothers.* In : Family Service Association of America, *Understanding the psychology of the unmarried mother*, New York
159. Young, L. R. (1947) *The unmarried mother's decision about her baby.* In : Family Service Association of America, *Understanding the psychology of the unmarried mother*, New York

NAME INDEX

SUBJECT INDEX

Abstract thinking impaired, 54, 55
Adaptivity retarded, 20
Adolescents
  in group care, 129
  in self-governing communities, 143
  retrospective studies, 15
Adoption
  administrative planning, 151
  agencies, 106
    See also Child-care agencies; Child-placing agencies
  follow-up studies needed, 107, 108
  illegitimate children, 96
  mother's decision, 102
  optimal age, 101-103
  period of waiting, cause of retardation, 103
  suitability of child, 104
Adoptive parents
  appraisal of, 104
  emotional experience, 106
  motivation, 104
  risks taken, 106
Adults, retrospective studies, 15
Affectionless characters
  See also Delinquents
  antecedent experiences, 47
  become psychopathic and unstable parents, 78
  craving for affection, 38
  discussed, 30-35
  institution children, 131
Agencies
  adoption, 106
  child-care, 111, 112, 114-116, 150, 151
  family welfare merging with child-placing, 150, 152
Aggression
  See also Aggressive characters; Aggressiveness
  in residential nurseries, 133
  of refugee children, 44
Aggressive characters, placement, 140

Aggressiveness
  See also Aggression; Aggressive characters
  of institution children, 39
  of maladjusted children, 142
  symptom in complex situation, 88
Aid to parents
  medical, 84, 87
  psychiatric, 91
  socio-economic, 85-87
Alcoholic parents, 122, 123
Amsterdam, day-schools for maladjusted children, 89
Animals as experimental subjects, 61
Anxiety
  as consequence of hostile feelings towards mother, 56
  as consequence of maternal deprivation, 49
  development discussed, 11
  learning toleration of, 57
  of children in hospital, 27
    delinquents, 13
    foster-children, 45
    goats, Liddell's experiment, 21
    mothers, 78
  on child's reunion with mother, 26
Apathy
  of foster-children, 44
  of residential-nursery children, 133
Austria, institution children studied in Vienna, 18

Babies, see Infants
Backwardness, see Retardation
Barcelona, neglected and delinquent children studied by Piquer y Jover, 45
Barnardo's Homes, psychopathic and unstable parents, 78
Bed-wetting
  See also Enuresis
  increased by evacuation, 28
  of foster-children, 45
  of refugee children, 44
  symptom in complex situation, 88

WORLD HEALTH ORGANIZATION
MONOGRAPH SERIES
No. 2

MATERNAL CARE AND
MENTAL HEALTH